THE ANALECTS OF CONFUCIUS
(*Lun Yu*)

THE ANALECTS OF CONFUCIUS
(*Lun Yu*)

A Literal Translation with an Introduction and Notes

by Chichung Huang

NEW YORK   OXFORD

Oxford University Press

1997

OXFORD UNIVERSITY PRESS

Oxford   New York   Athens   Auckland   Bangkok   Bogotá   Bombay
Buenos Aires   Calcutta   Cape Town   Dar es Salaam
Delhi   Florence   Hong Kong   Istanbul   Karachi
Kuala Lumpur   Madras   Madrid   Melbourne
Mexico City   Nairobi   Paris   Singapore
Taipei   Tokyo   Toronto

and associated companies in
Berlin   Ibadan

Copyright © 1997 by Chichung Huang

Published by Oxford University Press, Inc.,
198 Madison Avenue, New York, New York 10016

Oxford is a registered trademark of Oxford University Press, Inc.

Library of Congress Cataloging-in-Publication Data
Confucius.
[Lun yu. English]
The Analects of Confucius : Lun Yu /
A literal translation with an introduction and notes by Chichung Huang.
p. cm.   ISBN 0-19-506157-8 (cloth).—ISBN 0-19-511276-8 (paper)
I. Huang, Chichung.   II. Title.
PL2478.L513   1997   181'.11—dc20   96-24967

1 3 5 7 9 8 6 4 2
Printed in the United States of America
on acid-free paper

Dedicated to the memory of

my loving mother MRS. HUANG ZHAO XIUYING

（先慈黃趙秀英老大人）

and

my beloved daughter HUANG MAI（黃麥）

詩經·小雅　　(*The Book of Poetry, Minor Odes*)

蓼莪　　　THE TALL MUGWORT

蓼蓼者莪　How tall is the mugwort

匪莪伊蒿　That is not mugwort but wormwood!

哀哀父母　Alas, my father and my mother!

生我劬勞　Raising me, much did they suffer.

父兮生我　My father—he begot me;

母兮鞠我　My mother—she nursed me.

欲報之德　I wish to repay their bounty,

昊天罔極　The vast sky has no boundary.

ACKNOWLEDGMENTS

After a decade of researching, writing, and revising, I offer this new English version of *Lun Yu* as finally ready for print. I dare not claim it solely as my own work, for many are the scholars ancient and modern, Eastern and Western, who have contributed to its completion. First of all, I am immensely indebted to the major *Lun Yu* commentators, from the time of the Han Dynasty down to the present day, whose writings have greatly enhanced my comprehension of the text and the truthfulness of my translation. Thanks are also due to some of my predecessors in the translation of this monumental work, namely, Messrs. James Legge, Arthur Waley, D. C. Lau, James R. Ware, and Raymond Dawson, both the merits and the demerits of whose works have benefited my new rendition considerably. I wish to extend my special appreciation to three distinguished scholars who have read my manuscript with meticulous care and brought forth many constructive comments and suggestions. These are Dr. Shuen-fu Lin of the University of Michigan, the late Dr. Lucien Hanks, formerly of Bennington College, and Dr. Dominic LaRusso, professor emeritus at the University of Oregon. Others who deserve my heartfelt thanks for reading and improving my manuscript include Dr. Phebe Chao and Dr. Jane Hanks, formerly of Bennington College; Dr. Ben Kimpel, professor emeritus at Drew University; and Mrs. Karen Tsou of Portland, Oregon.

I am also much obliged to two former colleagues at Peking University: the late Professor Yang Zhou-han, who offered numerous insightful comments, and Professor Zhang Chuan-xi, who not only provided me with a good deal of biographical data unavailable in the United States but also shed much light on a number of controversial issues in interpretation. My deep gratitude also goes to Mrs. Rose Chiayin Tsou, a friend of long standing, whose contributions to my work are truly inestimable. As critic and voluntary typist, she has made many valuable proposals for improvement and typed my manuscript at least a dozen times over. Mr. Zhang Jin-shu, a former student of mine at

Peking University, also deserves my heartfelt thanks for proofreading the manuscript, procuring a number of bibliographical data, and proffering some sensible points in interpretation.

My deep appreciation also goes to the Smith Richardson Foundation, to Mrs. Dorothy Wallace, to Dr. and Mrs. Cyrus Gordon for their generous support, to Hamline University in St. Paul, Minnesota, for giving me the opportunity to offer the course on Lun Yu to its students, which germinated the idea of making a new translation, and to the University of Oregon in Eugene, Oregon, for granting me the privilege of using the fabulous collection of *Lun Yu* commentaries in the Orientalia Section of its library.

Last but not least, I am profoundly indebted to Mr. Scott Mahler, formerly sponsoring editor at the University of California Press in Los Angeles, and to Ms. Cynthia A. Read, senior editor at Oxford University Press in New York, for being the first individuals in the publishing world in the West to discover the merit of my work. Ms. Read is also responsible for improving its language.

CONTENTS

INTRODUCTION

For more than 2,400 years, the great majority of the Chinese, except
for a small number of Ru (Confucian) scholars, never even knew the
Master's real name, Kong Qiu; they always called him Kong Fuzi. Fuzi
was not part of his name but a title of respect applied to the ministers
at court in ancient times, equivalent to "Your Excellency" or "His
Excellency" in the English language. His disciples addressed him by
this title because he had once served as minister of justice in his native
state, Lu. Later, the title was applied to all teachers, and it gradually
picked up the connotation "master" or "teacher." So, to posterity,
Kong Fuzi means Kong the Master, or Master Kong. The name Confucius, by which he is widely known in the West, is a Latinized form
of Kong Fuzi; it was first used by four Roman Catholic missionaries
who in 1687 published at Paris a Latin translation of three Chinese
classics entitled *Confucius Sinarum Philosophus, sive Scientia Sinensis
Latine Exposita* (Confucius the Chinese Philosopher, or a Latin Ex-
position of Chinese Wisdom)[1] and has been vastly popular ever since.
In China, people sometimes also call him Kong Zi, a short form of
Kong Fuzi, which also means Master Kong, *zi* (which originally con-
noted "viscount") being a title of respect for men in general, like the
English word "Mister," a weakened form of "Master."

From the world's point of view, one would say that Master Kong's
life was a failure. What he had been yearning for all his life was to
take office and to implement the sage kings' way of government, or
humane government. At the age of fifty-one, he did take office, but
for only four or five years, in which he doesn't seem to have accomplished a great deal. He did win a diplomatic victory over the State of
Qi at the Jia-gu Assembly, but just as he was about to take measures
to weaken the power of the three usurping noble houses and to
strengthen the ducal house of Lu in the capacity of minister of justice,
he was obliged to resign from his post due to the infatuation of Duke
Ding, the then reigning prince of Lu, and his prime minister, Ji Huan-
zi, with a group of singing girls presented to them by the prince of Qi

with the intention of corrupting the court of Lu: surely enough the two neglected state affairs thereafter. The Master, disappointed, departed from his native land and, accompanied by a retinue formed by a number of his disciples, traveled through various states in search of a wise prince who would give him a chance to practice humane government, but for fourteen years he had no luck.[2]

Deplorable as his failure in government was, his successes elsewhere were beyond the wildest imagination of mortal man. Even when the Han historiographer Si-ma Qian (145–86? B.C.E.) wrote the glowing eulogy of the Master after concluding the latter's biography, he was able to visualize but a tiny fraction of the man's magnitude and his impact on the Chinese and on their civilization in the centuries to come. This is what Si-ma Qian said:

> "From kings to worthy men under Heaven, there have indeed been multitudinous! When they lived, they were glorified; when they died, they ceased to be. Master Kong was a commoner whose name has come down to us for more than ten generations[3] now, and who has been upheld by all scholars as their foremost teacher. Those who discourse on the Six Classics, including emperors, kings and marquises, all look upon the Master as their highest authority. He may be called the wisest indeed!"[4]

In as early as the third century B.C.E., long before Si-ma was even born, Master Kong's ethical teachings had already crossed the border of China and spread to Korea. From there, *The Analects* (*Lun Yu*) was brought to Japan by a Korean court academician named Wang Ren in the year A.D. 285.[5] And twenty-four centuries after Si-ma's death, the Master was hailed as "the greatest single intellectual force" among one fifth of the world's population.[6] As recently as January 1988, at a final session of the first international conference of Nobel prizewinners in Paris, the seventy-five participants, including fifty-two scientists, issued a list of sixteen conclusions after deliberating over four days on the theme "Facing the Twenty-First Century." The highlight of these conclusions is one that reads: "If mankind is to survive, it must go back 25 centuries in time to tap the wisdom of Confucius."[7]

In the long river of human history, if one single person can represent the civilization of a whole nation, it is perhaps Master Kong; if one single book can be upheld as the common code of a whole people, it is perhaps *Lun Yu*, or *The Analects of Confucius*. Many have wondered what it was in Master Kong the man or in his system or thought that has led to his paramount influence. In my view, his enduring impact may be attributed to two factors.

The first factor lies in the rational essence of his moral philosophy, the Way of humanity (*ren*). In defining the term *ren*, the Master said: "Loving men" (12.22). Love in the Master's ethical system is graded, rather than espousing equal love for all, as was advocated by his rival Mo Di, the leader of the Moist School. One loves one's parents more than any other people in the world; one loves one's kin more than strangers, more than even one's friends, and so on. This theory of graded love conforms not only to human nature but also to reason. For isn't that what everyone of us practices in our lives? So, in the Master's Way, love is conditioned by reason: It differs with the proximity or distance of every person we love. In fact, here, righteousness (reason) is the supreme criterion for all man's conduct and is therefore one of the most important virtues in the gentleman's self-cultivation, next only to humanity itself:

> Zi-lu said: "Does the gentleman uphold courage?"
> The Master said: "The gentleman regards righteousness as supreme. A gentleman who possesses courage but wants righteousness will become a rebel; a small man who possesses courage but wants righteousness will become a bandit." (17.22)

> The Master said: "A gentleman considers righteousness his essence: he practices it in accordance with the rituals, utters it in modest terms, and fulfils it with truthfulness. A gentleman indeed!" (15.18)

> The Master said: "The gentleman is conversant with righteousness; the small man is conversant with profit." (4.16)

A gentleman should uphold righteousness as his guiding principle in all human relations. Since we love people, we are obliged to help one another correct our mistakes. In a traditional Chinese family, the parents love their children, but they also discipline them. When a child does something wrong, the parents criticize her or him, sometimes even punish her or him. They don't "spare the rod and spoil the child," as is unfortunately widely practiced in China proper today due to the one-child policy. One loves one's parents more than any other people in the world, but when a parent does something wrong, one is supposed to remonstrate with her or him, although in a gentle way; if she or he does not accept one's advice, one should not get upset but should wait patiently for another chance. This critical attitude toward people we love applies to social relations as well. A minister is supposed to be loyal to the sovereign, but when the latter does something wrong, the minister is also supposed to remonstrate with him, often at the risk of his own life, and if the sovereign refuses to accept his advice, the minister should then leave office and look for a wise ruler to render his services. That's exactly what the Master himself did when he served as minister of justice in Lu (18.4). By the same token, we are supposed to be truthful to our friends, but if we have promised a friend to engage in a robbery or any other wrongdoing, we definitely should not keep such a promise, since it is not morally right. Righteousness is also the sole criterion advocated by the Master in our general attitude toward the world:

> The Master said: "the gentleman, in his attitude toward all under heaven, neither favors anyone, nor disfavors anyone. He keeps close to whoever is righteous." (4.10)

Many religious and philosophical theories have chosen love, or compassion, as their guiding doctrine, to wit, Buddhism advocates compassion (*cibei*); Christianity advocates love; Moism advocates equal love for all (*jian ai*); Taoism also advocates compassion (*ci*).[8] What makes Master Kong's Way of humanity uniquely distinctive is that it has enlisted righteousness (reason) as its criterion and supervising partner. Love is the best a person's heart can offer, and reason, the best a person's mind can offer. What ethical principle laid down by man could be more sensible than one that integrates the best one's heart can offer with the best one's mind can offer as the guiding light for one's conduct throughout one's life? Imagine that almost twenty-five centuries ago, in the hazy dawn of human civilization, Master Kong was already teaching his disciples to uphold rationalism even in their attitude toward the supernatural:

> When Fan Chi asked about wisdom, the Master said: "To apply yourself to the duties of man[9] and, while revering the spirits and gods, keep away from them. This may be called wisdom indeed." (6.22)

That is perhaps the reason that, twenty-two centuries later, when rationalism began to prevail in Europe during the Enlightenment, the French thinkers Voltaire, Diderot, and Quesnay and the German philosophers Leibnitz and Wolff praised the Master's moral philosophy and government theory so highly after reading *Lun Yu* and other classics of the Ru School.[10]

Although Master Kong upheld righteousness (reason) as the sole criterion for measuring man's conduct and discussed it repeatedly in the context of his ethical system, he himself never even once mentioned the two terms "humanity" and "righteousness" (*ren yi*) in one breath in *The Analects*, the book that records his words and deeds. It was two centuries later, when Mencius (Meng Zi), the Master's chief exponent, was interpreting and systematizing the Master's Way of humanity, that the two terms were first integrated into one doctrine, "the Way of humanity and righteousness" (*ren yi zhi dao*), which has become overwhelmingly more popular ever since than its original version, "the Way of humanity." In the very first chapter of his book *Mencius* (*Meng Zi*), he twice linked the two terms in one phrase that explicitly demonstrates the integration of love and reason in the guideline of Master Kong's moral philosophy.[11]

The Master's ethical theory is intertwined with his theory of government. He laid the foundation of his moral-political edifice on the family, believing that the terrible chaos of his day was brought about by the decline of the rituals, especially those governing human relations. He focused his attention on strengthening the virtues that govern human relations, especially family relations, believing that if every family could be brought to harmony, then there was hope that peace would eventually prevail in the empire, for eight out of the ten duties of man stipulated in *Li Ji* (*Records of the Rituals*) have to do with family relations:

> What are the duties of man? The father's lovingness and the son's filial piety; the elder brother's kindness and the younger brother's obedience;[12] the husband's dutifulness and the wife's compliance; the senior's beneficence and the junior's submissiveness; the sovereign's humaneness and the subject's loyalty. These ten are the duties of man.[13]

If every individual family member is well cultivated in the eight virtues that govern family relations, the family will surely become harmonious; if every family is harmonious, the state will surely become orderly; if every state is orderly, the empire will surely become peaceful. This whole program, which is more succinctly known as "Self-cultivation—family harmony—good order in the state—peace in the empire"[14] (*xiu shen—qi jia—zhi guo—ping tianxia*), makes prefect sense, and that is why the Master's theory of government based on the self-cultivation of the individual and on family harmony was so strongly supported by the emperors throughout Chinese history, as may be easily surmised from the following chapter, in which the disciple You Ruo expounded his master's teaching on this issue:

> Master You said: "Those who are filial to their parents and obedient to their elder brothers but are apt to defy their superiors are rare indeed; those who are not apt to defy their superiors but are apt to stir up a rebellion simply do not exist. The gentleman applies himself to the roots. Only when the roots are well planted will the Way grow. Filial piety and brotherly obedience are perhaps the roots of humanity, are they not?" (1.2)

To this day, the Master's family values still carry considerable binding force over people's lives in China and in the countries of Southeastern Asia, as well as wherever there is a congregation of Chinese population. Family ties, including marriage ties, are still cherished, though not quite so strongly as they used to be. Supporting the parents in their old age is still a son's or a daughter's undisputed duty. In fact, living with a son's or a daughter's family, a grandparent can be taken care of much better than in a nursing home, and she or he can do a much better job of taking care of and educating the grandchild(ren) than the day-care center can. The reason is simple and clear: There is genuine love involved in either case. The Master's teaching about revering the senior and esteeming the worthy (*jing lao zun xian*) is still upheld as a major societal virtue. To this day, the practice of offering sacrifices to one's deceased parents (and ancestors) at their graves is still observed in the countryside on several occasions a year, the significance of which is relevantly interpreted in *Li Ji*: "Offering sacrifices is meant to be the perpetuation of feeding one's parents and the continuation of filial piety."[15]

The second factor that contributes to Master Kong's enduring impact on Chinese civilization has to do with his age-long legacy of education. Prior to Master Kong's time, education was controlled by the court of the emperor and those of the various princes. Only children of the nobility were entitled to schooling; the children of commoners and serfs had no right to education. Books were also controlled by the officialdom; only children of the nobility had access to them. With the decline of the royal house of Zhou and the weakening of the feudal system in general toward the end of the Spring and Autumn period, the nobility began to lose its grip on some of its privileges, including that of education. To meet the needs of the time, private schools began to emerge on the scene. Master Kong's school was among the very first to accept children of the poor and the lowly:

> The Master said: "I instruct regardless of kind." (15.39)

> The Master said: "To anyone who spontaneously came to me with a bundle of dried pork, I have never denied instruction." (7.7)

> The Master said: "How worthy Hui is! Eating out of a bamboo container, drinking out of a gourd ladle, and living in a narrow shack— others would be utterly dejected, but Hui never alters his delight. How worthy Hui is!" (6.11)

Such disciples as Yan Hui, Zi-lu, Min Zi-qian, and Zeng Shen all came from poor and lowly families. In fact, only a handful, such as Meng Yi-zi, Nan-gong Jing-shu, Si-ma Niu, and Ru Bei, came from noble families. The Master was undoubtedly a pioneer in bringing education to the children of the common people. While the word "first" in his posthumous title "the first and wisest teacher" (*zhi shen xian shi*) stresses the idea "exemplary, or model," it also demonstrates time sequence. Many modern and contemporary scholars agree that he was one of the very first private scholar-teachers (*shi-ru*) and his school one of the very first private schools in Chinese history. There is little doubt, either, that his school of thought, the Ru School, was the first and foremost of "the hundred schools" and he, the forerunner of the various philosophers who emerged during the Pre-Qin period;[16] he was the only one active during the later part of the Spring and Autumn period, while the rest all appeared on the scene in the ensuing Warring States period, the earliest of them to appear being Mo Di, born around 478 B.C.E., shortly after the Master's death.[17] What makes it uniquely important, however is that his type of private school, in which the Six Arts and the Six Classics of the Ru School[17] were taught and where the cultivation of the student's virtues came before the acquisition of knowledge, gradually spread far and wide. At first, through the agency of the Master's own disciples, of whom Zeng Shen, Zi-zhang, Zi-xia, Zi-you, and others had all started schools of their own, disseminating the classics to various parts of the empire. Later, the Han emperor Wu

Di (156–87 B.C.E.) issued a decree upholding the philosophical system of the Ru School as the state orthodoxy to be taught in all schools of the empire and banning those of the other schools. Eventually, the private school system became the dominant form of education; its hegemony lasted well over two thousand years, until the turn of the twentieth century, when it began to make way for western-style schools. In the meantime, a set of imperial examinations based on the classics of the Ru School was designed to select the worthy and the talented to serve as officials at court as well as in the provinces. This system, set up during the reign of Emperor Yang Di (605–618) of the Sui Dynasty and abolished by Emperor Guang-xu of the Qing Dynasty in 1905, lasted about twelve to thirteen centuries. In short, Master Kong's moral philosophy, incorporated in the classics of the Ru School, was the basis for a whole civilization that was passed down from generation to generation through the private school system and the elite class (the officials and scholars who formed the intelligentsia of the time) and, by word of mouth and daily practice, was partially passed on through the elite class to the commoners, so that it has dominated the Chinese mind for the last twenty centuries. Much of it has long since merged into the Chinese tradition and is being practiced by the Chinese wherever they are, sometimes without their being aware of it.

Through the ages, Master Kong's ethical philosophy and the education system he initiated have also exerted some negative influences, of which two are of major importance. First, his ideas about the rituals, a code of propriety to regulate the actions of the people, allegedly laid down by King Wen and Duke Dan of the Zhou Dynasty, seem static, conservative, and at odds with the laws of evolution. He maintains that the rituals, which should be followed to the letter, no more and no less, as is stipulated by the doctrine of the constant mean, are always predictable in future dynasties:

> Zi-zhang asked: "Ten dynasties hence, are things predictable?"
> The Master said: "The Yin followed the rituals of the Xia; what has been reduced and augmented is known to us. The Zhou followed the rituals of the Yin; what has been reduced and augmented is known to us. Whoever may succeed the Zhou, even a hundred dynasties hence, things are predictable." (2.23)

The Master's judgment here apparently excludes drastic changes brought about by revolutions, radical reforms, and other unpredictable events. That is why his doctrine of the constant mean, which later evolved into a principle admonishing against going to excess in any action, was repeatedly made use of by emperors and princes to set back revolutions, revolts, reforms, and radical movements. As a result, the Master's conservative attitude in regard to the rituals, integrated with the theory of the constant mean and his advocacy of loyalty to the sovereign, played a major role in helping prolong considerably the lifespan of feudalism in China.

Second, the Confucian school system contributed to impeding China's progress in science and technology through the ages. In ancient China, schools were divided into two levels: elementary schools (*xiao xue*) and imperial colleges (*da xue*, or *tai xue*). During the Zhou Dynasty, the curriculum of the elementary schools comprised the Six Arts (*liu yi*), namely, the rituals, music, language, arithmetic, archery, and charioteering. During the Han Dynasty, it focused on the study of language and its correct reading (both in sound and meaning). From the Sui and Tang dynasties onward, it embraced philology, phonology and interpretation, as well as the rhyming system. In the imperial colleges, the curriculum centered on the intensive study of the Five Classics. In the Song Dynasty, *The Four Books* (*Si Shu*) were added to the curriculum of the imperial colleges by the renowned Confucian scholar Zhu Xi. They are *The Great Learning* (*Da Xue*), *The Constant Mean* (*Zhong Yong*), *The Analects of Confucius* (*Lun Yu*), and *Mencius* (*Meng Zi*). No courses in science and technology were ever offered, except a rudimentary presentation of arithmetic. Many contemporary scholars have ascribed China's backwardness in science and technology in modern times to the age-long absence of these courses in the curriculum of the Confucian school system, and rightly so. However, in my view, posterity, instead of shifting all the blame to the ancients, should take partial responsibility for the harm done, as the key to effecting change and progress lay in the hands of every generation.

Finally, a word about the title. The second character *yu* in the title *Lun Yu* is generally accepted to mean "dialogues," as the book records mostly Master Kong's dialogues with his disciples and contemporaries. The first character *lun* (with the word radical) means "to discuss" when pronounced in the fourth tone but when pronounced in the second tone, as it has been through the centuries, it is borrowed to function as *lun* (with the standing man radical) in the sense of *lunli,* meaning "ethical principles governing human relations" or, to be brief, "ethics, or ethical." Hence, *Lun Yu* is supposed to mean "Ethical Dialogues," which seems to make perfect sense and is completely in agreement with the contents of the book. Personally, I cannot think of a better reading for the two words that make up this title. However, as it has been the subject of controversy since the end of the Han Dynasty, I deem it proper to leave the interpretation open for discussion. The English word "analects" was first used by its pioneer British translator James Legge (1815–1897), of Oxford University, who explained his choice in a note on the title, saying: "I have styled the work 'Confucian Analects,' as being more descriptive of its character than any other name I could think of."[18] "Analects" originally means "literary gleanings." Though not exactly truthful to the original, the choice was apparently an immense success, for it has been used by almost every major translator who came along, and it seems to have become a tradition, if you will, a term specifically reserved for the rendition of *Lun Yu*. As such, it deserves to be honored.

NOTES

1. See *The Compact Edition of the Oxford English Dictionary* (London: Oxford University Press, 1971), p. 815. The three Chinese classics mentioned here are *Da Xue* (*The Great Learning*), *Zhong Yong* (*The Constant Mean*), and *Lun Yu* (*The Analects*).

2. Read pp. 195–96 in the Life of Master Kong.

3. Si-ma Qian died around 86 B.C.E., about 400 years after Master Kong's death in 479 B.C.E., roughly 13 generations earlier.

4. See *Shi Ji, Kong Zi Shi Jia* (*Records of the Historiographer, The Hereditory House of Master Kong*) (Beijing: Zhonghua Press, 1985), p. 1947.

5. See Kuang Ya-ming, *Kong Zi Ping Zhuan* (*A Critical Biography of Master Kong*) (Jinan: Qi-lu Press, 1985), p. 392.

6. See Huston Smith, *The Religions of Man* (New York: Harper & Row, 1964), p. 146.

7. See *Canberra Times*, Canberra, Australia, 24 January 1988.

8. See Wang Bi, *Lao Zi*, or *The Dao De Jing*, ch. 67, p. 15, in *Bai Zi Quan Shu* (*Complete Works of a Hundred Masters*), Tome VIII (Hangzhou: Zhejiang People's Press, 1985).

9. In *Lun Yu*, the term *yi* (righteousness) is sometimes rendered as "duty," in the sense of "what one ought to do." See the entry *yi* (righteousness) in the section on Terms, p. 18.

10. See Kuang Ya-ming, *Kong Zi Ping Zhuan* (*A Critical Biography of Master Kong*), pp. 400–405.

11. See D. C. Lau, *Mencius*, I.A.1. (London: Penguin Books, 1970), p. 49.

12. That the authority of elder brothers, especially the eldest brother, is stressed so much in Master Kong's ethical system is due to the feudal and patriarchal nature of Chinese society in his day. The eldest brother was the one to succeed the father as head of the family in the case of the latter's decease.

13. See *Li Ji, Li Yun* (*Records of the Rituals, The Evolution of the Rituals*) in *Shi San Jing Zhu Shu* (*Annotations and Interpretations on the Thirteen Classics*) (Beijing: Zhonghua Press, 1983), p. 1422.

14. See *Li Ji, Da Xue* (*Records of the Rituals, The Great Learning*) in *Shi San Jing Zhu Shu*, p. 1673.

15. See *Li Ji, Ji Tong* (*Records of the Rituals, The Essence of Sacrifice*) in *Shi San Jing Zhu Shu*, p. 1602.

16. The period in Chinese history before the book-burning campaign on orders from Qin Shi Huang Di (The First Emperor of Qin) in 213 B.C.E.

17. The Six Arts (Liu Yi): the rituals, music, language, arithmetic, archery, and charioteering (*li, yue, shu, shu, she, yu*). The Six Classics (*liu jing*)—only five of the six classics have come down to us: *The Book of Poetry* (*Shi Jing*), *The Book of History* (*Shu Jing*), *The Book of Rituals* (*Li Jing*), *The Book of Changes* (*Yi Jing*), and *The Spring and Autumn Annals* (*Chun Qiu*). Whether a book entitled *The Book of Music* (*Yue Jing*) ever existed is unknown to us. Some scholars maintain that such a book never existed; others believe that there was such a book, but it did not survive the book-burning campaign ordered by Qin Shi Huang Di (the First Emperor of Qin) in 213 B.C.E. That is why in later ages, they have come to be known as the Five classics (*Wu jing*).

18. See James Legge, *The Four Books* (Taipei: Jinchuan Press, 1973), p. 137.

TERMS

I THE WAY *(dao)*

Shuo Wen Jie Zi (*Interpreting Words and Analyzing Characters*), one of the earliest lexicons of the classical Chinese language, defines the character *dao* thus: "The road one walks on, composed of 'zhi' (to walk) and 'shou' (head), signifying 'that by which one walks all the way to one's destination' "; hence, a road or a way. From this root meaning is derived the connotation "a theory, doctrine, or body of principles upheld and followed by a group of believers." The English word "way" fits both the literal and the metaphorical meaning of the Chinese character nicely.

In *Lun Yu*, "the Way" stands for the Way of humanity, the supreme doctrine of Master Kong's philosophy. You Ruo, a prominent disciple, in expounding his master's Way, said: "The gentleman applies himself to the roots. Only when the roots are well planted will the Way grow. Filial piety and brotherly obedience are perhaps the roots of humanity, are they not?" (1.2). Here, he was virtually equating "the Way" with "humanity."

Sometimes, "the Way" is used by the Master to refer to the doctrine of wholehearted sincerity and like-hearted considerateness (*zhong shu*), or even like-hearted considerateness (*shu*) alone. For instance, Zeng Shen, another prominent disciple, in interpreting the Master's Way, said: "The Master's Way consists in wholehearted sincerity and like-hearted considerateness, that is all" (4.15). And when the disciple Zi-gong asked whether there was one single word that one could practice throughout one's life, the Master said: "It is perhaps 'like-hearted considerateness.' 'What you do not wish for yourself, do not impose on others' " (15.24). For in *Shuo Wen*, the lexicon mentioned earlier, the definition for the character *shu* is no other than *ren* (humanity). So, if one is able to practice either, one has undoubtedly attained the Way of humanity.

In *Lun Yu*, 1.12, we come across the phrase "the Way of the former kings." This refers to the Way of humane government allegedly implemented by the ancient sage kings Yao, Shun, Yu, Tang, Wen, Wu, and the Duke of Zhou.¹ Actually, the idea of humanity, or humane government was not initiated by Master Kong; he inherited it from these sage kings. Hence, *Li Ji, Zhong Yong* (*Records of the Rituals, The Constant Mean*) ch. 30 says: "Zhong-ni inherited the Way of Yao and Shun; he followed the institutions of Wen and Wu."² "The Way of Wen and Wu" in 19.22 was also part of the Way of the former kings, referring primarily to the rituals and institutions laid down by King Wen and his younger son, Duke Dan of Zhou.

As "the Way" represents humanity, the term "one who possesses the Way" (*you dao zhe*) means "a man of humanity" (*ren ren*), or, more often than not, "a ruler who implements humane government." Likewise, the term "one who has lost the Way" (*wu dao zhe*) means "a man of inhumanity" (*bu ren zhe*), or, more often than not, "a ruler who implements inhumane, or tyrannical government."

The word "way" (*dao*) is used by various philosophical schools in China to represent their respective systems of thought, especially by the Ru (Master Kong's) School and the Taoist (Lao Tzu's) School. For the former, the Way means a philosophical theory with humaneness, or humanity, as its guiding doctrine, whereas for the latter, the Way, often transliterated as the "Tao," or the "Dao," in English versions, means a naturalistic philosophy that advocates nonaction government in imitation of the evolution of nature, that is, by leaving the people the way they are and not using force to interfere with their lives.

2 VIRTUE *(de)*

In classical Chinese, the character for "virtue" (*de*) is interchangeable with that for "acquisition" (*de*), implying "that which one acquires in one's mind through cultivation," hence, "virtue, moral character, or moral force" as befits the context:

Zi-xia said: "In major *virtues,* one may not overstep the threshold; in minor *virtues,* some leeway is permissible." (19.11)

The Master said: "Since Heaven has endowed me with *moral force,* what can Huan Tui do to me?" (7.22)

Master Kong replied: ". . . The gentleman's *moral character* is the wind and the small man's *moral character,* grass. When grass is visited by the wind, it must surely bend." (12.19)

The word "virtue" (*de*) sometimes carries the force of "good quality":

> The Master said: "A thousand-*li* horse is praised not for its strength; it is praised for its *virtue*." (14.33)

In this context, "virtue" (*de*) refers to the quality of tameness. The English word "virtue" fits all these nuances well.

In order to implement humane government, the Master strongly advocates "rule by virtue and the rituals" instead of "rule by decrees and punishments," which means that, above all else, the ruler should be well cultivated in virtue himself so that he may set an example for the people to follow.

The minor virtues that appear in *Lun Yu* amount to fifty and more, among them filial piety, brotherly obedience, loyalty, sincerity, wholehearted sincerity, truthfulness, wisdom, reverence, devotion, gravity, awe, correction of error, gentleness, kindness, respectfulness, humility, deference, harmony, courtesy, righteousness, briskness in action, prudence in action, discretion in speech, straightness, dignity, courage, leniency, beneficence, like-hearted considerateness, staunchness, simplicity, refinement, integrity, lofty-mindedness, resoluteness, perception, moderation, constancy, broad-mindedness, uprightness, eruditeness, stamina, timeliness, clear-sightedness, far-sightedness, restraint, principledness, self-possessedness, expediency, gregariousness, truthfulness, four-squareness, and compliance.

3 HUMANITY *(ren)*

The character *ren* (humanity, or humaneness) is composed of two parts: a standing man on the left, *er* (two) on the right. *Shuo Wen* defines *ren* thus: "'Ren' means extensive love, hence the component 'two' (*er*)." In *Lun Yu*, 12.22, Master Kong's own definition of *ren* is "loving men." From its etymology, we may find two distinctive features of the word: (1) its close affinity to human beings; and (2) love on an extensive basis. The English word "humanity" (humaneness) seems to fit the foregoing features very well.

In Master Kong's ethical theory, humanity is the supreme virtue and the sum total of all virtues. As such, it is manifested in many aspects of human life. Hence, it is defined variously by the Master in *Lun Yu*:

1. In following the rituals:

> The Master said: "To restrain oneself and return to the rituals constitutes humanity.' . . ." (12.1)

2. In speech:

> The Master said: "The man of humanity speaks with hesitation." (12.3)

3. In one's attitude toward work:

> The Master said: "A man of humanity places hard work before reward." (6.22)

4. In government:

> Master Kong said: "To be able to practice five things under Heaven constitutes humanity."
> When further questioned about them, he said: "Respectfulness, lenience, truthfulness, industry, and beneficence." (17.5)

5. In treating others:

> The Master said: ". . . For a man of humanity is one who, wishing to establish himself, helps others to establish themselves, and who, wishing to gain perception, helps others to gain perception. . . ." (6.30)

Apart from being the supreme virtue and the sum total of all virtues, humanity sometimes represents a specific virtue required of a ruler, for a sage ruler is expected to embrace all the populace in his love. This may be seen from "the ten duties of man" prescribed in *Li Ji, Li Yun* (*Records of the Rituals, The Evolution of the Rituals*).[3]

As the supreme virtue and the sum total of all virtues, humanity is exceedingly difficult to attain. Being a modest man, Master Kong never accepted it for himself, nor would he accept it for any of his disciples (7.33, 5.5, 5.8). The only historical personages to whom he accorded this supreme virtue were the brothers Bo-yi and Shu-qi (7.14), the two young princes of the State of Gu-zhu; the Viscount of Wei, the Viscount of Ji, and Bi-gan (18.1), the three consuls and close relatives of King Zhou, the last emperor of the Yin Dynasty; and Guan Zhong, prime minister to Duke Huan of Qi (14.9, 14.16, 14.17), for bringing peace and order to the empire and his own state without using war chariots despite his deficiency in the rituals.

As people's relations with one another are different in degree, their love for one another is also different in degree. Hence, in Master Kong's ethics, love is graded according to the proximity and distance of each relationship. That is why Master Kong said: "Humanity is in human nature. The most important thing is to love one's kin."[4] Thus, one's love for the members of one's family and clan comes before that for people who are not related to one by blood. Likewise, within the family and clan, love for one's parents comes before that for any other member, and so forth. In other words, one does not extend equal love to everybody but gives to each his due as required by that specific relation stipulated by the rituals mentioned earlier. In this sense, Master Kong's theory of love is quite different from that of either Mo Di, founder of the Moist School during the Warring States period, who advocated equal love for all, or Christianity, which advocates equal love not only for everyone but also for one's enemy.

Master Kong gave much thought to the methodology of practicing humanity. He designed three major doctrines for that purpose, namely, the doctrine of wholehearted sincerity and like-hearted considerateness, the doctrine of the constant mean, and the doctrine of expediency. We shall discuss these doctrines one by one in due course.

4   RIGHTEOUSNESS (yi)

The character *yi* (righteousness) is composed of *yang* ("good," originally meaning "sheep") and *wo* ("me", meaning "what is good in me". *Ci Hai* (*Sea of Words*) defines it as "what is (morally) appropriate," hence, "righteousness," and by extension, "what one ought to do," "what is reasonable," or "duty," as befits the context:

> The gentleman regards *righteousness* as supreme. (17.22)

> To apply oneself to the *duties* of man and, while revering the spirits and gods, to keep away from them—this may be called wisdom. (6.22)

> The Master said: ". . . he employed the people *reasonably*." (5.16)

> The Master said: ". . . ; to see *something you ought to do* and not to do it is want of courage." (2.24)

In Master Kong's system of ethics, righteousness is next in importance only to humanity. He considers it the touchstone, the ultimate criterion for all human conduct, and all the virtues, too, including humanity:

The Master said: "The gentleman, in his attitude toward all under heaven, neither favors anyone, nor disfavors anyone. He keeps close to whoever is righteous." (4.10)

The Master said: "To love humanity and not to love learning⁵—the latent defect is foolishness; to love wisdom and not to love learning—the latent defect is unprincipledness; to love truthfulness and not to love learning—the latent defect is harmfulness; to love straightforwardness and not to love learning—the latent defect is impetuosity; to love courage and not to love learning—the latent defect is rebelliousness; to love staunchness and not to love learning—the latent defect is recklessness." (17.7)

There is no English word that can cover all these connotations, so I have to content myself with "righteousness."

In *Lun Yu*, whenever "the Way" appears in the text, the reader understands that it refers to the Master's Way of humanity. Master Kong himself never even once linked the concepts "humanity" and "righteousness" in one breath, not to mention calling his Way "the Way of humanity and righteousness." The first person to do so was Meng Ke (372?–289 B.C.E.), also known as Mencius (Meng Zi), the most prominent of his followers and interpreters, who was active almost two centuries after the Master's death generally acclaimed as the second sage of the Ru School. In the very first chapter of his book *Mencius*, he twice linked humanity and righteousness in one phrase, which was repeated numerous times throughout the book. "The Way of humanity and righteousness" has become more popular than "the Way of humanity" as the guiding doctrine of Master Kong's philosophy ever since.

5 THE RITUALS *(li)*

The character *li* is very graphic in its structural composition. The two parts that it comprises are *shi* (god) on the left and *li* (a ritual vessel) on the right, symbolizing the act of offering sacrifices to the gods, hence, the definition in *Shuo Wen*: "Practice, i.e., that by which one serves the gods to bring about blessings." The component *li* also contributes to the pronunciation of the word. By extension, the character *li* acquires two other connotations: "courtesy" and "gift." The English word seems to encompass all these ideas.

The rituals were a code of propriety, a set of rules and institutions by which people, or rather, those of the *shi* class (one between ministers and commoners, composed of minor officials and scholars) upward, were supposed to conduct themselves in their relations with the gods and spirits as well as with other human beings, hence, a code of propriety. This code of propriety encompassed all phases of human life, ranging from rituals governing state visits, organization of government institutions, state and family sacrifices, marriage, capping, mutual visits, banqueting, drinking parties, archery tournaments, learning, music, and mourning to etiquettes governing family and social relations and matters of dress, utensils, food, and so forth, all designed strictly in accordance with position and rank.

The rituals and music were used by good rulers as government measures to achieve humane rule—the rituals to regulate the people's actions, to bring security to the sovereign and good government to the people, and music, to harmonize their hearts, transform customs and modify conventions. To Master Kong, they were far superior to laws and punishments.

6   WISDOM, HUMANITY, AND COURAGE *(zhi, ren, yong)*

Li Ji, Zhong Yong, ch. 20 says: "Wisdom, humanity and courage—these three are the constant virtues under Heaven."[6] Therefore, in *Lun Yu*, wisdom and courage, like humanity, are characterized by a moral color, to be distinguished from worldly intelligence and daring.

In ancient texts, the character for "knowledge, or to know" (*zhi*, first tone) is often borrowed to function as "wisdom" (*zhi*, fourth tone). In early antiquity, as the Chinese language was not fully developed and there were not enough characters to go around, borrowing simpler characters to stand for more sophisticated ideas was a common practice.

In Master Kong's system of ethics, wisdom consists of three kinds of knowledge that a gentleman should possess:

> Master Kong said: "If one does not know the decree of Heaven, one has no way of becoming a gentleman. If one does not know the rituals, one has no way of establishing oneself. If one does not know speech, one has no way of knowing men." (20.3)

Like all other virtues, wisdom is subject to the scrutiny of the supreme criterion, righteousness, for otherwise, one may become conceited about one's wisdom and abuse it to engage in actions that go against righteousness.

To Master Kong, "courage" (*yong*) refers to the courage to do what is righteous, what is reasonable, or what one ought to do, that is, one's duty:

> The Master said: ". . . To see something you ought to do and not to do it is want of courage." (2.24)

The Master believes that the most courageous people are those who are ready to lay down their lives for the cause of humanity, such as the three lords of the Yin Dynasty who risked their lives in remonstrating against the tyrant Zhou for the good of the empire and its people (one of them did get killed due to his repeated remonstrations; see 18.1).

> The Master said: "Lofty-minded *shi* and humane men do not seek to preserve their lives at the expense of humanity; rather, they give their lives to attain humanity." (15.9)

Courage needs to be examined by the common criterion of righteousness, or the rituals, more than any other virtue. Any individual, whether gentleman or small man, who possesses courage but lacks the guidance of righteousness is likely to commit disastrous wrongdoings:

> The Master said: "A gentleman who possesses courage but wants righteousness will become a rebel; a small man who possesses courage but wants righteousness will become a bandit." (17.22)

7 WHOLEHEARTED SINCERITY AND TRUTHFULNESS
(*zhong xin*)

Sea of Words gives two definitions for the character *zhong*: wholehearted sincerity (*jie cheng*) and serving the sovereign even at the risk of one's life and, by inference, loyalty. The former is a general virtue in the ethical system of humanity, often integrated in the phrases "wholehearted sincerity and truthfulness" (*zhong xin*) and "wholehearted sincerity and like-hearted considerateness" (*zhong shu*); the latter is a specific virtue with which a subject is supposed to serve his sovereign:

> Master Zeng said: ". . . In counseling men, have I not been *wholeheartedly sincere?*" (1.4)

Master Kong replied: "The sovereign should employ the officials according to the rituals; the officials should serve the sovereign with *loyalty*." (3.19)

Loyalty as a subject's specific virtue in serving his sovereign is also regulated by righteousness in Master Kong's ethics. He does not advocate the kind of blind loyalty that prevailed in many later dynasties in China. His idea of loyalty requires a subject to offer advice and criticism to the ruler when the latter makes mistakes. And if the sovereign rejects them, the subject should then leave office (16.1), which is exactly what the Master himself did when he served as minister of justice in the court of Lu (see 18.4 and Life of Master Kong, p. 195).

The character *xin* (truthfulness) is composed of "a standing man radical" (*li ren*) on the left and "word" on the right, symbolizing a man standing by his word, hence, truthfulness, or trustworthiness. In a general sense, truthfulness is one of the two basic virtues under the Way of humanity, the other being wholehearted sincerity. In a narrow sense, it is a specific virtue of a friend in associating with his friends:

The Master said: ". . . He keeps wholehearted sincerity and *truthfulness* as his major principles, and does not befriend those beneath him." (1.8)

Master Zeng said: "In associating with friends, have I not been *truthful* to my word?" (1.4)

Truthfulness as a virtue is likewise subject to the scrutiny of the common criterion of righteousness:

The Master said: "Only when your truthfulness is close to righteousness can you keep a promise; . . ." (1.13)

To keep every promise indiscriminately without distinguishing whether or not the promise conforms to reason might be harmful. For instance, one definitely should not keep a promise with a friend to commit a murder or a theft.

Sincerity is the starting point of humanity. Wholehearted sincerity and truthfulness are therefore upheld as the two basic virtues of the Way of humanity. In *Lun Yu*, the Master repeatedly exhorts his disciples to keep wholehearted sincerity and truthfulness as their major principles (1.8, 9.25, 12.10). Equipped with these two basic virtues, he believes, one can get on in the world wherever one goes (15.6).

8 WHOLEHEARTED SINCERITY AND LIKE-HEARTED CONSIDERATENESS *(zhong shu)*

"Wholehearted sincerity and like-hearted considerateness" *(zhong shu)*, also known as "the doctrine of wholehearted sincerity and like-hearted considerateness" *(zhong shu zhi dao)*, is one of the three approaches to the Way of humanity, the other two being the doctrine of the constant mean *(zhong yong zhi dao)* and the doctrine of expediency *(quan dao)*. The first component, *zhong* (wholehearted sincerity), in this doctrine has already been discussed in the previous entry, *zhong xin* (wholehearted sincerity and truthfulness); the second component, *shu*, is also composed of two parts: the upper part, *ru*, meaning "same, or like," and the lower part, *xin*, meaning "heart"; integrated, they signify "(with) the same heart" or "like-hearted"; *Sea of Words* defines *shu* as "to think about and treat others as you would yourself" *(tui ji ji ren)*. According to the etymological structure of the word, I have rendered it "like-hearted considerateness." *Shuo Wen* defines *shu* directly as *ren* (humanity), implying that if one can think about and treat others as one would oneself, one has undoubtedly attained humanity. That is why in *Lun Yu*, *shu* is sometimes used to stand for *ren*. But in the collocation "wholehearted sincerity and like-hearted considerateness" *(zhong shu)*, it is integrated with "wholehearted sincerity" into a way to practice and attain humanity, just as the Golden Rule is a way to practice love in the Christian faith.

The doctrine of wholehearted sincerity and like-hearted considerateness has two aspects: the positive aspect and the negative aspect. The negative aspect admonishes people not to impose on others what they do not wish for themselves:

> Zi-gong asked: "Is there one single word that one can practice throughout one's life?"
> The Master said: "It is perhaps 'like-hearted considerateness.' 'What you do not wish for yourself, do not impose on others.'" (15.24)

The positive aspect encourages people to do to others what they wish for themselves:

> The Master said: "... For a man of humanity is one who, wishing to establish himself, helps others to establish themselves, and who, wishing to gain perception, helps others to gain perception. He is able to

take himself as an example. This may be called the approach to humanity." (6.30)

9   THE CONSTANT MEAN (zhong yong)

In *Li Ji, Zhong Yong* (*Records of the Rituals, The Constant Mean*), the Han commentator Zheng Xuan's note on the title of the book *Zhong Yong* says: "*Zhong Yong* is so entitled because it records the application of the mean; *yong* here means 'application.'" In his note on the same term in *Li Ji, Zhong Yong*, ch. 2, however, he says: "*Yong* means 'constant'; *zhong yong* means the application of the mean as a constant doctrine." The Wei commentator He Yan, in his note on the term *zhong yong* in *Lun Yu*, 6.29, says: "*Yong* means 'constant'; *zhong yong* means 'the mean as a constantly practicable virtue.'" He Yan's reading, which is also shared by Zheng Xuan, is followed by scholars through the ages; hence my rendition.

Very little explicit discussion on the term "the constant mean" (*zhong yong*) is found in *Lun Yu* itself. In the whole book, the complete form of the term appears only once where Master Kong merely uttered an exclamation of mixed praise and deploration for the constant mean as a virtue without touching upon its purport:

> The Master said: "The constant mean as a virtue is sublime indeed! People have been wanting in it for long!" (6.29)

The only equivocal discourse on the constant mean may be found in the following chapter between Master Kong and his disciple Zi-gong:

> Zi-gong asked: "Between Shi and Shang, which is worthier?"
> The Master said: "Shi goes beyond whereas Shang falls short."
> Zi-gong said: "Then, Shi is the superior?"
> The Master said: "To go beyond is the same as to fall short." (11.16)

The reader is totally at a loss as to what the Master and Zi-gong were talking about, for the object of the verb phrases "to go beyond" and "to fall short (of)" is nowhere to be found. However, the missing link is not far to seek. An episode in *Li Ji, Zhong-ni Yan Ju* (*Records of the Rituals, Zhong-ni at Leisure*) provides us with the necessary information:

> When Zhong-ni was at leisure, Zi-zhang, Zi-gong, and Yan You were standing in attendance. In their rambling conversation, they touched upon the rituals.

The Master said: "Be seated, the three of you. I shall discourse on the rituals for you so that you may apply the rituals correctly wherever you go."

Zi-gong stood up and asked: "May I venture to ask how?"

The Master said: "Reverence without conforming to the rituals is called boorishness; respect without conforming to the rituals is called suavity; courageousness without conforming to the rituals is called rebelliousness."

The Master said: "Suavity usurps compassion and humaneness."

The Master said: "Shi, you go beyond, and Shang falls short. Zi-chan was like a mother to the multitude. He was able to feed them, but unable to instruct them."

Zi-gong stood up and asked: "May I venture to ask what constitutes the mean here?"

The Master said: "The rituals! The rituals! The rituals are what constitutes the mean."[7]

So, what the constant mean signifies is following the rituals to the letter, no more and no less. Overdoing it and falling short of it are both shortcomings. In *Lun Yu*, the chapter that discusses the cultivation of a gentleman may shed some light on this doctrine:

The Master said: "When simplicity surpasses refinement, one is a rustic; when refinement surpasses simplicity, one is a scribe. Only when refinement and simplicity are well blended can one become a gentleman." (6.18)

Here, simplicity refers to one's native goodness of heart and refinement, to one's accomplishment in the rituals. The Master advocates a mean between native goodness of heart and accomplishment in the rituals for the self-cultivation of the gentleman. However, in the final analysis, simplicity is considered the essence of the rituals, hence, the more fundamental element of the two:

When Lin Fang asked about the essence of the rituals, the Master said: "What an enormous question! In the rituals, frugality is preferred to extravagance; in mourning, excessive grief is preferred to light-heartedness." (3.4)

Here, all four values are defects, for none conforms to the mean of the rituals. However, frugality and excessive grief are preferred to extravagance and light-heartedness because they stem from one's native goodness of heart—simplicity.

The idea of the mean as a moral as well as political doctrine was not initiated by Master Kong. The sage king Yao, in yielding the throne to his regent Shun, already said:

> "Hail, thou Shun! Heaven's decree of succession rests upon thy person. Faithfully adhere to *the mean* and thy rule shall extend to the Four Seas' ends; and Heaven's blessings shall last forevermore!" (20.1)

With the passing of time, the ancient rituals have receded to their proper place in history and become obsolete to modern man. The term "the constant mean" (*zhong yong*), too, has lost its original context and picked up the modern connotation "moderate," or "not going to excess."

10 EXPEDIENCY (*quan*)

The root meaning of the character *quan* is "weight," a piece of metal used in a steelyard as a standard of comparison in weighing. When we weigh something, we move that piece of metal back and forth to find the correct weight of the matter being weighed. *Shuo Wen* defines *quan* thus: "That which goes counter to the regular course." *Ci Hai* (*Sea of Words*) says: "It means 'change', changing the regular course to achieve the Way." As a doctrine in Master Kong's system of ethics, *quan* is defined by the Han commentators as "that which runs counter to the constant code of propriety to achieve the Way," "the constant code of propriety" here being the rituals. That is to say, in normal circumstances, one achieves the Way of humanity by practicing the rituals. However, in the event of a crisis or an unusual circumstance where practicing the rituals would prevent one from achieving humanity, one is obliged to depart from the rituals and take an expedient measure to reach the goal. The English word "expediency" seems to suit the context well. It is also known as "the doctrine of expediency" (*quan dao*), one of the three approaches to the Way of humanity, the other two being the doctrine of wholehearted sincerity and like-hearted considerateness and the doctrine of the constant mean. A classical example that illustrates the doctrine of expediency most aptly is offered in *Mencius*:

> Chun-yu Kun said: "A man and a woman are not supposed to give and take directly—this is prescribed by the rituals, is it not?"
> Master Meng said: "Yes, it is prescribed by the rituals."

Chun-yu Kun said: "If his sister-in-law is drowning, should he extend a helping hand to her?"

Master Meng said: "If his sister-in-law is drowning and he does not extend a helping hand to her, the man is a jackal, or a wolf. A man and a woman are not supposed to give and take directly—this is prescribed by the rituals; if his sister-in-law is drowning, he should extend a helping hand to her—this is prescribed by expediency."[8]

Expediency seems to be the most advanced and subtle doctrine in the methodology of Master Kong's Way of humanity and in the learning process of the Ru School:

The Master said: "Those who can learn with you may not be able to pursue the Way with you; those who can pursue the Way with you may not be able to establish themselves with you; those who can establish themselves with you may not be able to apply expediency with you."
(9.30)

It is believed that only one who is steeped in humanity and conversant with righteousness is able to apply the doctrine of expediency. Subtle and advanced as it is in the Master's system of thought, the subject is never discussed at any length or in any depth throughout *Lun Yu* except in two chapters (9.30, 18.8) where it is briefly mentioned without any discussion. If it were not for the example cited in *Mencius*, which illustrates the doctrine of expediency with such amazing lucidity, very few people would know what the doctrine was about. In fact, there are still a considerable number of Confucian scholars who know very little about its purport, its position and even its existence in Master Kong's ethical theory; some may never have heard its name.

Nevertheless, there is one striking example in *Lun Yu* that demonstrates the Master's dexterous application of expediency in evaluating the historical personage Guan Zhong, prime minister to Duke Huan of Qi. In 3.22, he censures Guan for violating the rituals in usurping the prince's prerogative of erecting a screen-wall in front of his gate and an earthen stand for returning drinking vessels in his entertaining quarters. Yet in 14.16 and 14.17 he unequivocally praises Guan as a man of humanity, an honor grudged many an otherwise highly accomplished gentleman, for his great achievements in assembling the princes of the various states nine times without the use of war chariots and for bringing peace and order to the whole empire as well as prosperity to his own state for close to half a century, thus making Duke Huan the first of the five overlords during the Spring and Autumn period. Few people in his position had made such enormous contributions to the people they ruled and served in Chinese history. The assessment of such a historical figure was a real dilemma to anyone who sat in judgment on him. It was only by applying the doctrine of expediency that the Master was able to free himself from such a predicament: A humane ruler or his aide was supposed to bring peace and prosperity to the people, the most humane thing he could ever achieve for them. Guan Zhong had brought such a felicity to his people for half a century, which is more than anybody could ask for. Yet he was arrogant enough to have usurped the prince's privileges, which was unforgivable under ordinary circumstances. Compared to his gigantic accomplishments, however, his errors were so dwarfed that they appeared to be insignificant. That is exactly why the Master accorded Guan the supreme virtue of humanity without reservation.

II FILIAL PIETY AND BROTHERLY OBEDIENCE *(xiao ti)*

The structure of the character *xiao* is remarkably illuminating: the upper part an abridged form of *lao* (old or old people), and the lower part, *zi* (son), symbolizing a son paying homage to and serving his parents down below, which demonstrates a son's love for his parents, hence, "filial piety."

Filial piety has been the paramount virtue governing human relations in China since time immemorial. Through Master Kong's promotion, it has reigned over Chinese society for more than twenty-five centuries. Hence, the motto "Filial piety is the first and foremost of all virtues" *(xiao wei bai shan xian)*.

Li Ji, Ji Tong (Records of the Rituals, The Essence of Sacrifice) prescribes the scope of filial piety thus: "Therefore, a filial son should serve his parents in three ways: to feed them when they are alive, to mourn them when they die and to offer sacrifices to them when mourning is over."[9] However, merely being able to perform these duties is not enough. The more important part of it is the love and reverence one feels for one's parents in one's heart. The practice of offering sacrifices to one's deceased parents and to earlier ancestors have persisted to this very day in China and other parts of the world where there is a Chinese community. The significance of such a practice is made very clear in *Li Ji, Ji Tong (Records of the Rituals, The Essence of*

Sacrifice): "Sacrifice is meant to be the perpetuation of feeding one's parents and the continuation of filial piety."[10]

Filial piety is also subject to the scrutiny of righteousness. When one's parents make mistakes, one is also supposed to offer them advice and criticisms, but in a very gentle manner. If the advice is rejected, one should not be impatient and resentful but should wait for another opportunity. The parent-and-child relationship, like all other human relationships, is reciprocal in nature: While the child should be filial to his or her parents, the parents should be loving to the child.

The character *ti* (brotherly obedience) is also composed of two parts: a *shu xin* (vertical heart) radical on the left and *di* (younger brother) on the right, signifying a younger brother's love for his elder brother. *Sea of Words* defines *ti* as "obedience," implying a younger brother's obedience to his elder brothers, especially the eldest one.

Although *ti* (brotherly obedience) is mentioned only three times in *Lun Yu*, and always in the wake of its infinitely more imposing forerunner "filial piety," it is nonetheless considered one of the two basic virtues in family relations, the reason being that seniority in the family, especially that of the eldest brother, who was entitled to succeeding the father as head of the family when the latter passed away, held a very important position in the patriarchal clan system of the day. The relationship between brothers is also reciprocal, of course: While the younger brother should be obedient to his elder brothers, the elder brothers should be kind (*liang*) to their younger brothers.

Filial piety and brotherly obedience not only constitute the cornerstone of the family system but also lay the foundation for good government in the state and peace in the empire. For they help shape young people into loyal and law-abiding subjects. By the same token, a ruler who is well cultivated in filial piety, paternal love, brotherly kindness will surely become a role model for the people to imitate.

All this is in tune with Master Kong's master plan of humane government: "self-cultivation—family harmony—good order in the state— peace in the empire" (see p. 9).

12 REFINEMENT AND SIMPLICITY *(wen zhi)*

Shuo Wen defines the character *wen* thus: "*Wen* is composed of crisscross lines, symbolizing a colorful composition," and, by extension, "refinement." Both *Sea of Words* and *Sources of Words* (*Ci Yuan*) define *zhi* as "pu" (simplicity); in Master Kong's ethics, it implies native goodness of heart, the basis of humanity. Refinement and simplicity are the two qualities that contribute to the making of a gentleman, a man of talent and virtue: Refinement stands for his accomplishment in the rituals, and simplicity, for his native goodness of heart; according to the Master, a gentleman must possess both to merit that name, and, what is more, the qualities should be proportionately blended. In other words, a gentleman must strike a mean between simplicity and refinement.

In the final analysis, however, simplicity is the underlying component and the more essential of the two in the gentleman's self-cultivation (see 3.4, 7.35).

13   RESPECTFULNESS AND REVERENCE *(gong jing)*

The characters *gong* and *jing* are used together as a composite term meaning "respect(ful)" nowadays. When used separately in ancient texts, *gong* means "respectful(ness)" and *jing*, "reverence, or reverent." *Shuo Wen* defines both "gong" and "jing" as "respectful(ness)." *Sea of Words* has a clear-cut definition for either member of the composite term: "What is expressed in appearance is *gong* (respect); what is cherished in the heart is *jing* (reverence). In general usage, *gong* and *jing* have the same meaning." This note applies to the two terms used in *Lun Yu* very nicely. Here, *gong* (respectfulness) generally implies keeping a dignified and neat appearance as well as an affable and modest attitude, and *jing* (reverence), a very dignified attitude accompanied by heartfelt esteem. This difference may clearly be seen from the following examples:

> The Master said: "The only one who achieved good government without doing anything was perhaps Shun. For what did he do? He conducted himself respectfully (*gong*) facing due south, that is all." (15.5)

> The Master said: "Nowadays filial piety merely means being able to feed one's parents. Even dogs and horses are being fed. Without reverence (*jing*), how can you tell the difference?" (2.7)

The character *jing* sometimes is also used to show one's conscientious attitude toward work and is translated as "devotion" or "devoted."

"Respectfulness" is also regulated by righteousness, or the rituals. For if one carries it to excess, one's attitude will become subservient, and people will despise one for it. That is why the Master said: "Sweet words, a pleasing countenance, and excessive respectfulness—Zuo Qiuming deems it shameful; I also deem it shameful . . ." (5.25).

14 SAGE MEN *(sheng ren)*

As the character *ren* (man) in *Lun Yu* often stands for a member (or members) of the nobility, ranging from an emperor to a county magistrate, "sage men" generally means "sage kings." In the tradition of the Ru School, the sage kings refer to seven wise rulers of antiquity who allegedly governed by the rituals and music, thus achieving humane government: King Yao of Tang, King Shun of Yu, King Yu of Xia, King Tang of Shang, King Wen of Zhou, King Wu of Zhou, and Duke Dan of Zhou. (See note 1.) Each was the supreme ruler of his empire, the only exception being Duke Dan of Zhou, who assisted his elder brother King Wu in founding the Zhou Dynasty and ruled as prince regent for his young nephew King Cheng after King Wu's death, laying down the official system and institutions of the Zhou Dynasty. Thus, although he was not a king, he actually served in the capacity of a supreme ruler for seven years before his nephew was old enough to take over.

After Master Kong's death, the followers of the Ru School applied the title "the sage man" to their master, the founder of their school, the only person who was addressed as "the sage man" without the official title of "king" or the like.

In 1.12, we find the term "the former kings" *(xian wang)*, which is widely used in ancient texts as an equivalent of "the sage kings," for the character *wang* (king) in classical Chinese generally implies a good ruler. Hence, the term "the Way of the former kings" *(xian wang zhi dao)* in the same chapter is equivalent to "the Way of the sage kings" or "the sage kings' Way of humane government," identical with the Way of humanity that Master Kong inherited from the sage kings and developed into a whole system of philosophy.

15 BENEVOLENT MEN *(shan ren)*

The term *shan ren* (a benevolent man) appears in four chapters of *Lun Yu*. From the contexts of all four, the term should read "a benevolent prince" and not "a benevolent man" as is upheld by the Wei commentator He Yan and others in 7.25, where Master Kong was deploring that the Way was on the decline, so he would have no chance to see either a sage king or a benevolent prince emerge in his lifetime. That "a benevolent man" means a benevolent prince is self-evident, for instance, in the following chapter:

> The Master said: " 'If benevolent men were to rule a state a hundred years, they would be able to tame brutes and abolish capital punishment.' How true this saying rings!" (13.11)

16 DUKEDOM, MARQUISATE, EARLDOM, VISCOUNTCY, AND BARONAGE *(gong, hou, bo, zi, nan)*

The ancient sage kings instituted five ranks for the nobility of the emperor's court, namely, dukedom *(gong)*, marquisate *(hou)*, earldom *(bo)*, viscountcy *(zi)*, and baronage *(nan)*,[11] which are identical with the Western system. Of these five, the rank "duke" appears a number of times in *Lun Yu*, mostly in the titles of the princes of the various states, such as "Duke Ai of Lu" and "Duke Ling of Wei." For the prince of a state to call himself "duke" was apparently a usurpation, for most princes of states in those days were marquises, and those of smaller states were only earls, viscounts, or even barons. Not one of them had officially been granted the title "duke" by the emperor. As usurpation was the vogue of the day, the princes of the seven states of the Warring States period—Qin, Qi, Zhao, Yan, Wu, Yue, and Chu—all usurped the title "king" one after another while the king of the Zhou Dynasty was still presiding over the empire. The rank "viscount" appears only twice in 18.1, in the titles "the Viscount of Wei" and "the Viscount of Ji," two of the three lords who remonstrated against the tyrant Zhou toward the end of the Yin Dynasty. The other three ranks—marquis, earl, and baron—never appear in *Lun Yu*.

17 CONSULS, MINISTERS, AND *SHI* *(qing, daifu, shi)*

During the Zhou Dynasty, the court of the various states consisted of three levels of officials: consuls *(qing)*, ministers *(daifu)*, and *shi*. Each level is again divided into three grades: senior consuls *(shang qing)*, middle consuls *(zhong qing)*, and junior consuls *(xia qing)*; senior ministers *(shang daifu)*, middle ministers *(zhong daifu)*, and junior ministers *(xia daifu)*; senior *shi* *(shang shi)*, middle *shi* *(zhong shi)*, and junior *shi* *(xia shi)*. The *shi* were a class of people between ministers *(daifu)* and commoners *(shuren)*, composed of minor officials and scholars. The English terms "consul" and "minister" seem to fit the Chinese terms *qing* and *daifu* quite well, but it is very difficult to find a suitable equivalent in English for the Chinese term *shi* with its complicated implications. Hence, I have decided to use the transliterated form of the character and provide a note for it.

When the Master served as minister of justice in Lu, he held the title of "consul," for it is stipulated in the *Zhou Li* (*The Rituals of the Zhou Dynasty*), also known as *the Zhou Guan*, (*The Official System of the Zhou Dynasty*) that the Ministry of Justice is to be held by a consul.[12]

In one chapter alone, the word *shi* is used to mean "office" or "duties":

> The Master said: "If wealth and rank could be sought, be it a whip-holder's office, I would take it. If it cannot be sought, I shall follow my liking." (7.11)

18   THE GENTLEMAN, THE SMALL MAN (*junzi, xiaoren*)

The term *junzi* literally says "a king's son" and, by extension, "a member of the nobility (or officialdom)." This was what it meant during the greater part of the Zhou Dynasty. Toward the end of the Spring and Autumn period, *junzi* gradually picked up a new connotation— "one who is erudite in learning, retentive in memory, yielding, and applying himself to good deeds without slackening," or "a man of talent and virtue," which last connotation has become dominant ever since. In *Lun Yu*, the term is used in four different meanings. In most cases, it refers to a man of talent and virtue (15.18); sometimes, it retains its original meaning—a member of the nobility or officialdom (19.10). Occasionally, in its third sense, it stands for the emperor or the prince of a state (18.10), and once in a while, it is used by the disciples to refer to Master Kong (19.9).

What are the qualities that go into the making of a gentleman (a virtuous and talented man)? A proportionate blending of simplicity (native goodness of heart) and refinement (fine accomplishment in the rituals):

> The Master said: "When simplicity surpasses refinement, one is a rustic; when refinement surpasses simplicity, one is a scribe. Only when refinement and simplicity are well blended can one become a gentleman." (6.18)

The term "gentleman" (*junzi*) appears more than a hundred times in *Lun Yu*, and many virtues are attributed to him. Apparently he is meant to be the ideal man in Master Kong's Land of Grand Concord (*datong shijie*), equivalent to "man of humanity" (*renren*) or "one who possesses the Way" (*youdaozhe*).

The term *xiaoren* literally says "small men" and, by inference, "commoners." This was what it meant during the greater part of the Zhou Dynasty. Toward the end of the Spring and Autumn period, *xiaoren* gradually picked up a new connotation—a mean and unvirtuous man, which has become its dominant meaning ever since. In *Lun Yu*, however, sometimes the term retains its original meaning—commoners. In either sense, it serves as the opposite of the gentleman. The gentleman and the small man are contrasted explicitly and implicitly in at least twenty chapters in this book, but the major demarcation line lies in righteousness and profit: The gentleman's chief concern in life is righteousness, whereas the small man's is profit.

19   THE SCHOLAR-TEACHER *(ru)*

In antiquity, the character *ru* referred to a category of people who were originally sorcerers, scribes, sacrifice-officiators and fortune-tellers and later to those who served as masters of ceremonies in the performance of rituals for the *shi* and the nobility at such events as weddings, funerals, and sacrifices. Subsequently, the semantic evolution of the character *ru* passed through three other stages: During the Zhou Dynasty, it was applied to scholar-teachers (*shiru*) who instructed the classics (or one of the classics); when the Ru Confucian School came into being after Master Kong's death, *ru* took on the new connotation "a member of the Ru School"; when the Ru School began to dominate education and academic learning in China, the term *ru* came to represent scholars in general until the turn of the twentieth century.

In *Lun Yu*, the term appears only twice in the same chapter:

> The Master said to Zi-xia: "You be a gentleman *ru* and not a small man *ru*." (6.13)

At this juncture, Zi-xia had started a school of his own. So, the Master advised him on the kind of teacher he should become. The Qing commentator Liu Bao-nan says: "A gentleman *ru* understands great things and undertakes great responsibilities; a small-man *ru* applies himself only to petty and shallow things. The gentleman and the small man here are differentiated by capacity and not by inclination."

20 MEN AND PEOPLE *(ren, min)*

The everyday word *ren* (man) has two different connotations in *Lun Yu*: an ordinary man and a member of the nobility (or the officialdom). That *ren* carries the force of a nobleman can be seen clearly from the following:

> When Zi-lu asked about the gentleman, Master Kong said: "He culti-vates himself in bringing peace to *men*."
> Zi-lu said: "Is that all?"
> The Master said: "He cultivates himself in bringing peace to the hundred family names." (14.42)

By contrast, it is clear that "men" here refers to the nobility, and "the hundred family names," to the common people.

There are plenty of instances in *Lun Yu* that verify this point beyond a doubt: "A sage *man*" means "a sage king"; "a benevolent *man*," "a benevolent prince"; "great *men*," "the emperor and the princes of the various states"; and "the *man* of Zou County," the magistrate of Zou County, Master Kong's father Shu-liang He.

The character *min* generally means "people." Other terms that con-vey the same idea are "the hundred family names" (*baixing*) and "the multitude" (*zhong*).

NOTES

1. Yao—see 6.30, note 1; Shun—see 6.30, note 2; Yu—see 8.18, note 2; Tang—see 12.22, note 2; King Wen—see 9.5, note 2; King Wu—see 8.20, note 1; Duke Dan of Zhou—see 7.5, note 1.
2. See *Shi San Jing Zhu Shu* (*Annotations and Interpretations on the Thir-teen Classics*) (Beijing: Zhonghua Press, 1983), p. 1634.
3. Ibid., p. 1422.
4. Ibid., p. 1629.
5. "Learning" here refers to the learning of the rituals.
6. See *Shi San Jing Zhu Shu*, p. 1629.
7. Ibid., p. 1613.
8. See *Mencius*, IV.A.17.
9. See *Shi San Jing Zhu Shu*, p. 1603.
10. Ibid., p. 1602.
11. Ibid., p. 1321.
12. Ibid., pp. 867, 2757.

A COMPARATIVE CHRONOLOGY

502?   *Gong-shan Fu-rao rebels against Ji-sun and summons Master Kong*

501   Defeated, Yang Huo escapes to Qi, Song, and Jin

       Master Kong appointed magistrate of Zhong-du

  ?   *Master Kong visits the court of Zhou, learns the rituals from Lao Tan and music from Chang Hong*

500   *Master Kong promoted to deputy minister of public works, and later to minister of justice*

       At the Jai-gu Assembly, Master Kong defeats Qi's conspiracy to abduct Duke Ding of Lu

498   *Master Kong's plan to demolish the city walls of the three Huans' fiefs is unsuccessful*

497   Duke Ding and Ji Huan-zi accept singing girls from Duke Jing of Qi

       Master Kong departs from Lu and arrives in Wei

496?   Birth of Sophocles in Greece

       Master Kong is besieged at Kuang

       Master Kong's audience with Nan-zi

493   *Master Kong's peril in Song*

490   The Greeks defeat the Persians at Marathon

489   *Master Kong's party is besieged between Chen and Cai and runs out of food for seven days*

       Master Kong's visit to Chu

       Duke She consults the Master on statecraft and the rituals

485   *Death of Master Kong's wife*

484   Birth of Herodotus in Greece

       Ran You defeats Qi's invasion at Qing

       Master Kong returns to Lu at Ji Kuang-zi's request

483?   Death of Siddhartha Gautama in India

       Death of Master Kong's son Li

       Birth of Master Kong's grandson Zi-si

481   *Master Kong stops editing the Spring and Autumn Annals*

       Death of Master Kong's favorite disciple, Yan Yuan

GUIDE TO PRONUNCIATION

The transliterations of all Chinese terms and proper names in this book follow the Chinese phonetic system, generally known to the world as the pinyin system. Basically identifiable with their counterparts in the International Phonetic Alphabet, its consonants are easily pronounceable with the exception of a few which were endowed by their inventor(s) with sound values different from the ones they usually represent in the English language. Readers of this book are advised to familiarize themselves with these sounds so that they are not impeded by them in pronouncing Chinese words throughout this book. They are as follows:

c	= ts	as in	pu*ts*
q	= ch	as in	*ch*ew
x	= sh	as in	*sh*ark
z	= dz	as in	nee*ds*
zh	= j	as in	*j*aw (a rough equivalence)

Chinese Vowels and Diphthongs

Chinese phonetic symbols	International phonetic symbols	Chinese example	English example
a	[a]	Da-xiang	calm
o	[o]	Bo-yi	pot
e	[ə]	She	le (Fr.)
i	[i]	Bo-yi	sheep
u	[u]	Lu	root
ü	[y]	Qu Bo-yu**	rue (Fr.)
-i	[ŋ] [ʅ]*	Ci, Chi	---
er	[ər]	Zhong-er	further

Chinese phonetic symbols	International phonetic symbols	Chinese example	English example
ai	[ai]	Tai-bo	bite
ei	[ei]	Ru Bei	take
ao	[au]	Gao Yao	out
ou	[əu]	Shou-yang	row
an	[an]	Fan Chi	---
en	[ən]	Chen	chosen
ang	[aŋ]	Chang	---
eng	[əŋ]	Teng	---
ong	[uŋ]	Gong	---
ia	[ia]	Xia	---
ie	[iɛ]	Jie-ni	pied (Fr.)
iao	[iau]	Qi-diao Kai	---
iu, iou	[iəu]	Qiu	you
ian	[ian]	Dian	---
in	[in]	Lin Fang	din
iang	[iaŋ]	Xiang	---
ing	[iŋ]	Duke Ding	ping-pong
iong	[yŋ]	Yong	---
ua	[ua]	Zi-hua	---
uo	[uə]	Yang Huo	poor
uai	[uai]	River Huai	why (wai)
ui, uei	[uei]	Huan Tui	---
uan	[uan]	Guan Zhong	---
un, uen	[uən]	Shun	---
uang	[uaŋ]	Kuang	---
üe	[yɛ]	Xue	---
üan	[yan]	Yuan Si	---
ün	[yn]	Xun	---

Notes:*[ɿ] is used after z, c, s; [ʅ] is used after zh, ch, sh, r.
**The umlaut (¨) is omitted but understood after j, q, x, y.

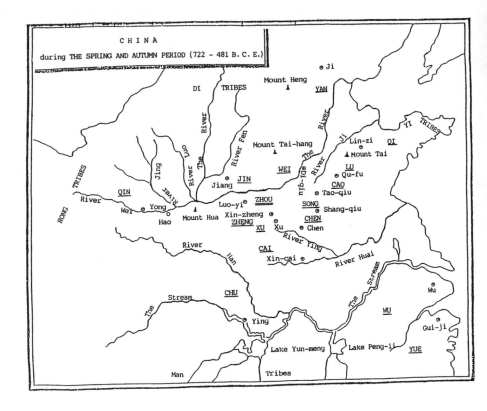

C H I N A

during THE SPRING AND AUTUMN PERIOD (722 - 481 B.C.E.)

The Empire, the States, and Their Capitals

State	Capital
CAI	Xin-cai
CAO	Tao-qiu
CHEN	Chen
CHU	Ying
JIN	Jiang
LU	Qu-fu
QI	Lin-zi
QIN	Yong
SONG	Shang-qiu
WEI	Di-qiu
WU	Wu
XU	Xu
YAN	Ji
YUE	Gui-ji
ZHENG	Xin-zheng
ZHOU (the empire)	Hao (West Zhou)
	Luo-yi (East Zhou)

Non-Chinese Tribes

YI TRIBES	(to the east of China)
MAN TRIBES	(to the south of China)
RONG TRIBES	(to the west of China)
DI TRIBES	(to the north of China)

Rivers and Lakes

RIVER FEN

RIVER HAN

RIVER HUAI

RIVER JI

RIVER JING
RIVER LUO
THE RIVER   (Huanghe, or the Yellow River)
THE STREAM, (or the Jiang)   (Changjiang, or the Yangtze River)
RIVER WEI
RIVER YING
LAKE PENG-LI
LAKE YUN-MENG

Mountains

MOUNT HENG
MOUNT HUA
MOUNT TAI
MOUNT TAI-HANG

THE ANALECTS OF CONFUCIUS
(Lun Yu)

Book One

XUE ER *(To Learn Something And)*

1.1 The Master[1] said: "To learn[2] something and[3] regularly practice it—is it not a joy? To have schoolfellows come from distant states—is it not a pleasure? Not to resent when men do not know you—is it not like a gentleman?"[4]

> 1. Master Kong (see Life of Master Kong).
> 2. Note that learning in *Lun Yu* has a special connotation implying both the cultivation of virtue and the acquisition of knowledge, with special emphasis on the former.
> 3. As a rule, the first two or three characters (often after the introductory phrase "The Master said,") of the first chapter of each book are used as the title of that book.
> 4. A man of virtue and talent.

1.2 Master You[1] said: "Those who are filial to their parents and obedient to their elder brothers but are apt to defy their superiors are rare indeed; those who are not apt to defy their superiors, but are apt to stir up a rebellion simply do not exist. The gentleman applies himself to the roots. Only when the roots are well planted will the Way[2] grow. Filial piety and brotherly obedience are perhaps the roots of humanity,[3] are they not?"

> 1. You Ruo, one of Master Kong's prominent disciples.
> 2. The Way of humanity, the supreme doctrine of Master Kong's moral philosophy.
> 3. All-embracing love as the supreme doctrine of Master Kong's Way.

1.3 The Master said: "Sweet words and a pleasing countenance have indeed little humanity in them!"[1]

> 1. Cf. 5.25, 17.16.

1.4 Master Zeng[1] said: "I daily thrice examine myself. In counseling men, have I not been wholeheartedly sincere? In associating with friends, have I not been truthful to my word? In transmitting something, have I not been proficient?"

>   1. Zeng Shen, one of Master Kong's prominent disciples.

1.5   The Master said: "In governing a thousand-chariot state,[1] be reverent to your duties and truthful; economize expenditure and love men; employ the people at proper times."[2]

>   1. In ancient times, because battles were conducted on chariots, the military power of a state was measured by the number of chariots it possessed. A thousand-chariot state during Master Kong's time was a fairly small one. (See 11.24.) Note that each chariot was drawn by a team of four horses.
>   2. I.e., during slack seasons in farming.

1.6   The Master said: "Younger brothers and sons should be filial to their parents at home, obedient to their elder brothers abroad,[1] discreet and truthful, love all the multitude and keep close to humane men. If, after practicing these, they have energy to spare, they should employ it to acquire culture."[2]

>   1. "Abroad" here implies "at school."
>   2. The Six Arts, namely, the rituals, music, archery, charioteering, language, and arithmetic.

1.7   Zi-Xia[1] said: "He who loves worthy men instead of beautiful women;[2] who, in serving his parents, can exert all his energy; who, in serving the sovereign, can exhaust his talent; and who, in associating with friends, is truthful to his word—although others may say he has not learnt, I will surely say he has learnt."

>   1. Alias of Bu Shang, one of the Master's prominent disciples.
>   2. A variant reading says: "He who, in choosing a wife, values her virtue more than her beauty."

1.8   The Master said: "If a gentleman is not grave, he will not be awe-inspiring. If he learns, he will not be benighted.[1] He keeps wholehearted sincerity and truthfulness as his major principles and does not befriend those beneath him.[2] When he makes a mistake, he is not afraid to correct it."[3]

1. Ignorant about the rituals. A variant reading of this sentence is: ". . . and what he learns will not be solid."

2. I.e., inferior to him in virtue.

3. Cf. 9.25.

1.9 Master Zeng said: "Show genuine grief at a parent's death,[1] keep offering sacrifices to them as time goes by, and the people's moral character shall be reinforced."

1. This was said about a ruler.

1.10 Zi-qin asked of Zi-gong:[1] "When the Master arrives in a certain state, he always learns about its government. Does he seek it,[2] or is it offered to him?"

Zi-gong said: "The Master obtains it through gentleness, benevolence, respectfulness, frugality, and deference.[3] The way the Master seeks it is perhaps different from the way others seek it, is it not?"

1. These are aliases of Chen Kang and Duan-mu Ci, two of the Master's major disciples. The latter was very prominent in statecraft and diplomacy.

2. Information about its government.

3. This concise and ambiguous sentence implies that the Master obtained the information by observing the customs of that state to see if the people thereof were gentle, benevolent, respectful, frugal, and deferential as a result of having been instructed in the spirit of the Six Classics, namely, *The Book of Poetry, The Book of History, The Book of Rituals, The Book of Music, The Book of Changes*, and *The Spring and Autumn Annals*. (See *Shi San Jing zhu Shu*, p. 1609.)

1.11 The Master said: "When his father was alive, he observed his aspirations; when his father died, he observed his deeds. If, for three years, he does not change his father's Way,[1] he may be said to be filial."[2]

1. His father's humane way of government.

2. This is said in regard to a filial son, a prospective ruler. (Cf. 4.20.)

1.12 Master You said: "In the application of the rituals,[1] harmony[2] is most valuable. Of the Way of the former kings,[3] this is the most beautiful part. However, if matters small and great all follow them, sometimes it will not work.[4] But if you keep pursuing harmony just because you know harmony, and do not use the rituals to regulate it, it will not work either."[5]

1. The rituals were a code of propriety that governs all phases of human life, including self-cultivation, personal conduct, and etiquettes governing family and social relations, state affairs, and sacrificial rites.

2. Being the effect of music, harmony stands for music here. The rituals and music were major government measures employed by humane rulers in ancient China, the former to regulate the people's actions, the latter to harmonize their feelings. Hence, performance of the rituals was always accompanied by music, sometimes by dance too. (Cf. 3.1, 3.2, 3.3.)

3. Referring to King Wen, King Wu, and Duke Dan of Zhou (see "Sage Men" in Terms, p. 31.)

4. That is, without the harmonizing effect of music, the people would find the rituals too rigid. "Them" stands for the rituals here.

5. This is a discussion on the constant mean between the rituals and music.

1.13   Master You said: "Only when your truthfulness is close to righteousness can you keep a promise; only when your respectfulness is close to the rituals can you keep humiliation away; only when you love those akin to you are you worthy of esteem."

1.14   The Master said: "The gentleman,[1] in eating, does not seek satiety; in dwelling, does not seek comfort. He is brisk in action and discreet in speech.[2] He goes to those who possess the Way for rectification. Such a man may be said to love learning indeed."

1. A man of virtue.
2. Cf. 2.13, 4.22, 4.24, 12.3, 14.20, 14.27.

1.15   Zi-gong said: "A man who is poor but does not flatter, or rich but does not swagger—what do you think of him?"

The Master said: "Commendable, but not so good as one who is poor but delights in the Way,[1] or rich but loves the rituals."

Zi-gong said: "*Poetry*[2] says:

'Like carving, like filing;
Like chiseling, like polishing.'[3]

Is this what it means?"

The Master said: "Ci,[4] I can begin to discuss *Poetry* with you now. For when I tell you what is past, you know what is to come."[5]

1. The prevalent texts have "who is poor but happy" where older texts have "who is poor but delights in the Way." I follow the latter.

2. *The Book of Poetry.*

3. Lines from *The Book of Poetry, Ballads of the State of Wei, The Bend of River Qi.* The similes signify that, in learning, a scholar should seek progress unceasingly, like an artisan who carves, files, chisels, and polishes a piece of precious stone until perfection is reached.

4. Given name of Zi-gong.

5. "What is past" refers to what the Master had said earlier, and "what is to come," to Zi-gong's quotation from *The Book of Poetry* as a supplement to the Master's reply.

1.16 The Master said: "Do not worry about men[1] not knowing you; rather, worry about incapability and ignorance."[2]

1. People in high positions.

2. Prevalent texts read: ". . . rather, worry about your not knowing men." (Cf. 4.14, 14.30, 15.19.)

Book Two

WEI ZHENG *(He Who Conducts Government)*

2.1 The Master said: "He who conducts government with virtue may be likened to the North Star, which, seated in its place, is surrounded by multitudes of other stars."[1]

> 1. The simile implies a virtuous ruler who, seated in his court and guiding the nation with his own moral excellence, is revered and obeyed by all the people.

2.2 The Master said: "The three hundred poems[1] in *Poetry* may be covered in one phrase: " 'Without deviating.' "[2]

> 1. *The Book of Poetry* actually contains 305 poems; 300 is the round number.
> 2. This line appears in *The Book of Poetry, Hymns of the State of Lu, Stalwart Horses*, quoted here by the Master to imply that the poems in *The Book of Poetry* do not deviate from the right path—the Way of the sage kings.

2.3 The Master said: "If you govern them with decrees and regulate them with punishments, the people will evade them but will have no sense of shame. If you govern them with virtue and regulate them with the rituals, they will have a sense of shame and flock to you."

2.4 The Master said: "At fifteen, I bent my mind on learning; at thirty, I was established;[1] at forty, I was free from delusion;[2] at fifty, I knew the decree of Heaven;[3] at sixty, my ears became subtly perceptive;[4] at seventy, I was able to follow my heart's desire without overstepping the rules of propriety."

> 1. I.e., well accomplished in the rituals. (See 8.8, 16.13, 20.3.)
> 2. Well accomplished in the rituals and highly cultivated in virtue, the Master was free from delusion at forty. (Cf. 9.29, 14.28.)
> 3. The Master knew even then that the sage kings' Way of humane government was not to prevail.

4. On hearing what a man said, he immediately understood his subtle implications.

2.5   When Meng Yi-zi[1] asked about filial piety, the Master said: "Do not act contrary."[2]

When Fan Chi[3] was driving, the Master said to him: "When Meng-sun[4] asked me about filial piety, I replied: 'Do not act contrary.'"

Fan Chi said: "What do you mean?"

The Master said: "When your parents are alive, serve them in accordance with the rituals; when they die, bury them in accordance with the rituals; offer sacrifices to them in accordance with the rituals."

1. Posthumous title of Zhong-sun He-ji, minister of Lu, one of Master Kong's major disciples. Note that in ancient China, when a noble man or an official died, he was granted a posthumous title according to the deeds he had performed during his lifetime.

2. When the verb *wei* (to act contrary to or violate) is used absolutely in ancient Chinese texts, its object is usually understood to be "the rituals," as may be inferred from the rest of the chapter.

3. Alias of Fan Xu, one of Master Kong's major disciples.

4. Meng-sun (also known as Zhong-sun), compound family name of Yi-zi, often shortened to Meng.

2.6   When Meng Wu-bo[1] asked about filial piety, the Master said: "As for your parents, what you should worry about most is their illness."[2]

1. Posthumous title of Zhong-sun Zhi, son to Meng Yi-zi, minister of Lu and then head of the noble house of Meng-sun.

2. Two variant readings are: "Let your parents worry about nothing except your illness" and "What your parents worry about you most is your illness."

2.7   When Zi-you[1] asked about filial piety, the Master said: "Nowadays filial piety merely means being able to feed one's parents. Even dogs and horses are being fed. Without reverence, how can you tell the difference?"[2]

1. Alias of Yan Yan, one of Master Kong's major disciples.

2. A variant reading of this sentence is: "Even dogs and horses can serve men."

2.8 When Zi-xia asked about filial piety, the Master said: "Facial expression is most difficult.[1] When there are chores, the younger brothers and sons render their services; when there is wine and food, the seniors drink and eat. Can this alone be considered filial piety?"

>   1. The most difficult thing for the filial son is to maintain a cheerful expression. A variant reading is: "The difficult thing is to serve your parents according to their facial expressions."

2.9 The Master said: "Once I talked with Hui[1] all day; he never contradicted me, as if stupid. When he retired, I observed him in private and found that he was able to elucidate. Hui is not at all stupid."

>   1. Yan Hui, one of Master Kong's prominent disciples.

2.10 The Master said: "See what a man does;[1] contemplate the path he has traversed;[2] examine what he is at ease with. How, then, can he conceal himself? How, then, can he conceal himself?"

>   1. Other possible readings of this clause are: "See what a man's motive is . . ." and "See the company one keeps. . . ."
>   2. That is, what he has done all along. Other readings of this clause are: "See what a man's motive is . . ." and "See what a man's ways and means are. . . ."

2.11 The Master said: "He who keeps reviewing the old[1] and acquiring the new[2] is fit to be a teacher."

>   1. What one has already learned; the classics.
>   2. What one has not learned; up-to-date knowledge. (Cf. 19.5.) A variant reading is: "He who keeps reviewing old lessons and thereby acquires something new is fit to be a teacher."

2.12 The Master said: "The gentleman is not a utensil."[1]

>   1. A utensil usually has only one use; the metaphor represents a man who is specialized in one branch of learning or one skill and thus can serve only one purpose. According to Master Kong, a gentleman should be well accomplished in virtue and widely informed in the classics so that he may assume great responsibilities.

2.13 When Zi-gong asked about the gentleman, the Master said: "His action goes first; his speech then follows it."[1]

> 1. Cf. 1.14, 4.22, 4.24, 12.3, 14.20, 14.27.

2.14 The Master said: "The gentleman is all-embracing and not partial; the small man is partial and not all-embracing."[1]

> 1. The gentleman embraces all in his extensive love; the small man is partial to a few for selfish purposes.

2.15 The Master said: "Learning without thinking is fruitless;[1] thinking without learning is perplexing."[2]

> 1. Variant readings of this clause are: "Learning without thinking leads to deception; . . ." and "Learning without thinking leads to misunderstanding the sage kings' Way; . . ."
> 2. Variant readings of this clause are: ". . . ; thinking without learning leads to weariness" and ". . . ; thinking without learning leads to danger." (Cf. 15.31.)

2.16 The Master said: "To apply oneself to heretical theories[1] is harmful indeed!"[2]

> 1. Referring to the theories of the various schools other than that of the Ru (Confucian) School.
> 2. The Master exhorted the disciples to devote themselves wholeheartedly to pursuing the Way of humanity.
> Variant readings of this chapter are:
> "To apply yourself to different trades and skills is harmful indeed" and "Attack the heretical theories and their harm shall cease."

2.17 The Master said: "Iou,[1] do you understand what I have taught you?[2] If you understand it, say you understand it. If you do not understand it, say you do not understand it. This is wisdom."[3]

> 1. Given name of Zi-lu, one of Master Kong's prominent disciples.
> 2. A variant reading of this sentence is: "Iou, shall I teach you what is meant by 'knowing something?' "
> 3. A variant reading of this sentence is: "This is true knowledge."

2.18 When Zi-zhang[1] asked how to seek an official's salary, the Master said: "Hear[2] much, leave out what is doubtful, discreetly speak about the rest, and you shall make fewer mistakes. See[2] much, leave out what is hazardous, discreetly practice the rest, and you shall have fewer regrets. If you make fewer mistakes in speech and have fewer regrets in action, an official's salary lies therein."

1. Alias of Zhuan-sun Shi, one of Master Kong's major disciples.

2. In *Lun Yu*, sometimes "to hear" and "to see" both carry the force of "to learn."

2.19 Duke Ai[1] asked: "What must we do to make the people obedient?"

Master Kong replied: "Promote the upright, place them above the crooked, and the people shall be obedient. Promote the crooked, place them above the upright, and the people shall be disobedient."

1. Posthumous title of the then reigning prince of Lu (r. 494 B.C.E.–466 B.C.E.) (Cf.12.22.)

2.20 Ji Kang-zi[1] asked: "How do you make the people reverent, loyal, and mutually encouraging?"

The Master said: "If you preside over them with dignity, they will be reverent; if you are filial and loving,[2] they will be loyal; if you promote the good and instruct the incapable,[3] they will be mutually encouraging."

1. Posthumous title of Ji-sun Fei, then head of the noble house of Ji-sun and prime minister of Lu.

2. I.e., filial to your parents and loving to your children.

3. Incapable of good.

2.21 Someone said to Master Kong: "Sir, why do you not participate in government?"

The Master said: "*History*[1] says: 'How exceedingly filial you are! And how kind to your younger brothers![2] You can extend this to the officialdom.'[3]—That is also participating in government. Why must one personally participate in government?"

1. *The Book of History*, one of the Six Classics, the earliest history of China.

2. A quotation from *The Book of History, History of the Zhou Dynasty, Jun Chen* (See *Shi San Jing Zhu Shu*. p. 236.)

3. Here, King Cheng of Zhou was commending his minister Jun Chen.

2.22　The Master said: "If a man is not truthful, I do not know how he can get along. A big cart without the hinges,[1] or a small cart without the pins[2]—how can one make it run?"

> 1. Movable wooden pegs with an iron coating for fastening the horizontal bar of an ox-cart to the front ends of its shafts.
> 2. The same kind of wooden pegs used for the same purpose on a smaller cart drawn by a horse.

2.23　Zi-zhang asked: "Ten dynasties hence, are things predictable?"[1]

The Master said: "The Yin followed the rituals of the Xia; what has been reduced and augmented is known to us. The Zhou followed the rituals of the Yin; what has been reduced and augmented is known to us. Whoever may succeed the Zhou, even a hundred dynasties hence, things are predictable."[2]

> 1. Zi-zhang was asking about possible alterations in the rituals of future dynasties.
> 2. The Xia, the Yin (or Shang), and the Zhou are known as The Three Dynasties in the dawn of Chinese history.

2.24　The Master said: "To offer sacrifices to spirits other than those of your own ancestors is flattery.[1] To see something you ought to do and not to do it is want of courage."[2]

> 1. Such people were trying to seek blessings from these spirits by flattering them with sacrifices.
> 2. In Master Kong's ethics, courage means bravery to do what is righteous, or what one ought to do (one's duty).

Book Three

BA YI *(Eight Rows of Dancers)*

3.1　Master Kong said of Ji Shi:[1] "Eight rows of dancers[2] danced in his court. If this could be tolerated, what could not be tolerated?"

> 1. Head of the noble house of Ji-sun. The character *shi* means family name (xing). Here, it indicates that his family name was Ji. When used with a man, it denotes one of rank and distinction, when used with a woman, it denotes her maiden name.
>
> 2. Only the emperor was entitled to eight rows of dancers for a total of 64 at a sacrificial ceremony in his ancestral temple; a prince, six rows of eight (48); a minister, four rows of eight (32); a *shi* (a minor official), two rows of eight (16). So Ji Shi was usurping the emperor's prerogative.

3.2　The men of the three houses[1] removed the offerings singing *Harmony*.[2]
　　　The Master said:

> " 'Assisted by the various princes,
> The Son of Heaven[3] stands reverent and majestic.'[4]

How could this apply to the hall[5] of the three houses?"

> 1. The three noble houses in control of state power in Lu, namely, those of Meng-sun, Shu-sun, and Ji-sun, often shortened to Meng, Shu, and Ji, respectively, the house of Ji being the most powerful of them all.
>
> 2. A song based on the words of a poem from *The Book of Poetry, Hymns of the Zhou Dynasty*, used exclusively by the emperor at the conclusion of a sacrificial ceremony in his ancestral temple.
>
> 3. The emperor regarded Heaven as his father, Earth as his mother, and himself as the son of Heaven.
>
> 4. Lines from the hymn *Harmony*, describing the emperor solemnly offering sacrifices to his ancestors, attended by the princes of the various states.
>
> 5. The sacrificial hall in their ancestral temple.

3.3　The Master said: "If a man[1] is not humane, what can he do with the rituals? If a man is not humane, what can he do with music?"[2]

  1. "Man" here refers to the sovereign.
  2. For the rituals and music, (see 1.12 notes 1 & 2.)

3.4 When Lin Fang[1] asked about the essence of the rituals, the Master said: "What an enormous question![2] In the rituals,[3] frugality is preferred to extravagance; in mourning, excessive grief is preferred to light-heartedness."[4]

  1. One of Master Kong's major disciples.
  2. If one understands the essence of the rituals, one understands the whole colossal institution of the rituals that governs man's public life and personal life; hence, an enormous question.
  3. Referring to auspicious and festive ceremonies such as a state celebration or a wedding.
  4. Here, the Master discoursed on the constant mean in the application of the rituals. Extravagance and excessive grief go beyond the prescriptions of the rituals, whereas frugality and light-heartedness fall short of them. Therefore, all four are defects. However, as frugality and excessive grief stem from simplicity (innate goodness of heart), they are preferred to extravagance and light-heartedness, for the essence of the rituals lies in simplicity.

3.5 The Master said: "Even the Yis and Dis[1] have regard for their sovereigns, unlike the various states of Xia,[2] which have none."[3]

  1. *Yi* is an ancient name for the non-Chinese tribes to the East of China proper, and *Di*, for those to its North. "The Yis and Dis" is often used to represent all the non-Chinese tribes on the borders of China.
  2. An ancient name for China, meaning "great."
  3. The Master was censuring the three noble houses of Lu, as well as those in the various states, for usurping state power.

3.6 When Ji Shi[1] was about to perform the Display Sacrifice[2] at Mount Tai,[3] the Master said to Ran You[4]: "Can you not stop it?"
  Ran You replied: "No, I cannot."
  The Master said: "Alas! Is it possible that Mount Tai is not as good as Lin Fang?"[5]

  1. Here referring to Ji Kang-zi, then prime minister to Duke Ai of Lu.
  2. The name of a sacrificial ceremony to the god of a mountain, a prerogative of the prince, so called because sacrificial animals and articles of jade were first displayed on tables and then buried in the earth as sacrifices to the guardian god of the mountain.

3. The first and foremost sacred mountain in China, located in the present-day Shandong Province.

4. Alias of Ran Qiu, one of Master Kong's prominent disciples, then serving as Ji Kang-zi's chief house officer.

5. Implying that the God of Mount Tai certainly knew better about the essence of the rituals than Lin Fang and naturally would not accept Ji Kang-zi's presumptuous offerings.

3.7   The Master said: "Gentlemen have nothing to contend for. If an exception must be cited, it is perhaps in archery.[1] They cup their hands[2] and yield the way to each other before ascending and descending.[3] Then they drink. Even in contention, they are gentlemanly."

1. A ritual archery tournament.

2. An ancient form of salutation performed by cupping one's right hand in the left.

3. Ascending and descending the stairs leading to the tournament hall.

3.8   Zi-xia asked:

" 'Dimpled are her charming smiles!
Crystal-clear are her beautiful eyes!
To a white ground are added colours bright.'[1]

What does it mean?[2]"
      The Master said: "Painting comes after a white ground."[3]
      Zi-xia said: "So the rituals come after too?"[4]
      The Master said: "Shang,[5] you are the one to elucidate my ideas! I can begin to discuss *Poetry* with you now."

1. This is generally believed to be a lost poem, although the first two lines can still be found in *The Book of Poetry, Ballads of the State of Wei, A Beautiful Lady*. The third has been lost. (See *Shi San Jing Zhu Shu*, p. 322.)

2. Zi-xia, in reading the poem, did not quite understand the metaphor in the third line; hence the query.

3. A metaphor meaning that a lady must first have natural good looks before cosmetics can enhance her beauty. This in turn means figuratively that simplicity comes before refinement, or humanity comes before the rituals.

4. On hearing the Master's reply, Zi-xia immediately comprehended the essence of the metaphor. When he suggested it to the Master, the latter was overjoyed at Zi-xia's quick understanding.

5. Zi-xia's given name.

3.9 The Master said: "The rituals of the Xia,[1] I can discourse on them. I went to Qi,[2] but they could not provide enough evidence. The rituals of the Yin,[3] I can discourse on them. I went to Song,[4] but they could not provide enough evidence, either.[5] That is because they did not have enough literature and worthy men left. If they did, I would be able to prove it."

> 1. The rituals instituted by the sage king Yu, founder of the Xia Dynasty.
>
> 2. A small state descended from the Xia Dynasty, in what is now Qi County, Henan Province.
>
> 3. The rituals instituted by the sage king Tang, founder of the Shang (or Yin) Dynasty.
>
> 4. A small state descended from the Yin Dynasty, in what is now Shangqiu, Henan Province.
>
> 5. The division of the previous sentences follows the text of a similar account in *Li Ji, Li Yun (Records of the Rituals, The Evolution of the Rituals)* in *Shi San Jing Zhu Shu*, p. 1415.

3.10 The Master said: "What comes after the first libation in the Di Sacrifice,[1] I have no wish to observe."[2]

> 1. *Di*, signifying "discreet," was an eminently important sacrificial ceremony held once every five years by the emperor to honor all his royal ancestors. At this ceremony, the wooden tablets representing the spirits of all his ancestors were assembled in the temple of the founding father of the dynasty to share the offerings. It was so named because special discretion in arranging the order of the various tablets in accordance with the lineage of the royal house was emphasized.
>
> 2. First, the right to perform the Di Sacrifice, a prerogative of the emperor, was granted to Lu upon the founding of the state to honor Duke Dan of Zhou, its founding father, who had rendered meritorious services to the founding of the Zhou Dynasty. However, for Lu to continue observing the ritual was a usurpation; furthermore, the order of the tablets was not properly arranged. Hence the Master's aversion to witnessing the ceremony.

3.11 Someone asked the purport of the Di Sacrifice. The Master said: "I do not know.[1] He who knows its purport will find the affairs under Heaven as if displayed here."[2] And he pointed at his palm.

> 1. In saying he did not know, the Master was trying to avoid discussing the subject. For it was prescribed by the rituals that a subject should avoid discussing the sovereign's faults in public.
>
> 2. I.e., clear and easy to understand. Note that "under Heaven" here means in the empire.

3.12   When offering sacrifices,[1] he felt as if the spirits were present; when offering sacrifices to the gods, he felt as if the gods were present.
The Master said: "If I did not participate in a sacrifice, it would be as if no sacrifice had been offered."[2]

> 1. "To the spirits of his ancestors" is implied.
> 2. This chapter demonstrates the Master's reverence in offering sacrifices to the gods and the spirits of his ancestors.

3.13   Wang-sun Jia[1] asked: " 'It is better to flatter the Kitchen God[2] than to flatter the Interior God.'[3] What does it mean?"[4]
The Master said: "It is not so. If one has sinned against Heaven, there is no one to pray to."[5]

> 1. Minister of military affairs to Duke Ling of Wei.
> 2. A household deity who is believed to keep a record of both the good and the evil deeds of each member of the household and to go up to report them to the God of Heaven on the last day of each moon. To this day, he is still worshipped in the Chinese countryside. Here, it is a metaphor representing the most influential minister in the State of Wei, i.e., Wang-sun Jia himself.
> 3. A metaphor implying Nan-zi, the duke's wife, who was closest to the duke and influential in state affairs as well. This is believed to be a popular saying of the time.
> 4. By asking the Master the meaning of this common saying, Wang-sun was insinuating that the Master would do better to flatter him than even someone like Nan-zi, who was closer to the duke than he.
> 5. With this, the Master declined Wang-sun's advice to flatter him or anyone else. "Heaven" here is a metaphor representing Duke Ling of Wei.

3.14   The Master said: "The Zhou, as compared with the two previous dynasties,[1]—how magnificent is its culture![2] I follow the Zhou!"

> 1. The Xia and the Shang (or Yin) dynasties.
> 2. "Culture" here refers to the rituals and institutions established by King Wen and Duke Dan of Zhou.

3.15   When the Master entered The Founding Father's Temple,[1] he inquired about everything. Someone said: "Who says the son of the man of Zou County[2] knows the rituals? When he entered the Founding Father's Temple, he inquired about everything."[3]
The Master, on hearing this, said: "Such are the rituals."[4]

1. Also known as Duke of Zhou's Temple, the duke being the founding father of Lu. (See 7.5, note 1.)

2. The man of Zou County refers to Shu-liang He, Master Kong's late father, who had served as magistrate of Zou County in his day.

3. The Master was known as an accomplished scholar in the rituals; hence the sarcasm.

4. That is, the rituals were such matters that should be treated with the utmost reverence and discretion. (Cf. 10.15.)

3.16   The Master said: " 'Archery does not stress penetrating the hide.'[1] For manual labor was divided into different levels.[2] Such was the way of the ancients."[3]

1. The Master was discussing ritual archery here, which stressed not only hitting the leather target but also gentle deportment and rhythmic movement. In his day, the rituals were on the decline, and the vogue in ritual archery stressed penetrating the leather target alone.

The quotation was taken from *Yi Li, Xiang She Li (Ceremonial Rituals, Rituals Governing Prefecture Archery Tournaments*, see *Shi San Jing Zhu Shu*, p. 1011). (Cf. 3.7.)

2. In ancient times, manual labor was divided into three levels according to the intensity of exertion.

3. In commending the ancients for upholding the rituals, the Master was censuring his contemporaries for advocating force.

3.17   Zi-gong wanted to dispense with the raw sheep for the prayer ceremony on the first day of each moon.[1] The Master said: "Ci, you grudge your sheep; I grudge my rituals."[2]

1. According to the rituals, at the end of each year, the emperor was supposed to issue an official calender for the coming year to the princes of the various states, stipulating the first day of each moon and the government measures that went with that moon. On receiving this calendar, each prince was to put it in his founding father's temple for safekeeping; on the first day of each moon the following year, he was to pray at the temple with a raw sheep as sacrifice, take out the list of government measures designated for that moon; and put them into execution. This practice had been suspended in Lu for a long time; yet the functionary in charge of the ceremony still provided a raw sheep for the occasion. Hence Zi-gong's wish to dispense with it.

2. The presence of the sheep would still remind people of the prayer ceremony, while its absence would mark its abolition. Hence the Master's wish to keep it. This episode might have occurred when Zi-gong was in office in Lu.

3.18 The Master said: "He who serves the sovereign fully in conformity with the rituals is considered by others a flatterer."[1]

> 1. In the Master's day, most people ignored the rituals in serving the sovereign. Therefore, they considered those who followed the rituals flatterers.

3.19 Duke Ding[1] asked: "The sovereign employing the officials, the officials serving the sovereign—how should it be done?"[2]

Master Kong replied: "The sovereign should employ the officials in accordance with the rituals; the officials should serve the sovereign with loyalty."

> 1. Posthumous title of Ji Song, then reigning prince of Lu (r. 509–495 B.C.E.).
> 2. During this period, as the duke's subjects ignored the rituals in serving him, he was concerned. Hence the query.

3.20 The Master said: *"The Melodious Chirping of the Fish Hawks* is joyous but not wantonly so, melancholy but not injuriously so."[1]

> 1. The Master praised *The Melodious Chirping of the Fish Hawks*, the first poem of *The Book of Poetry, Ballads of the Various States*, and its music for abiding by the constant mean in the expression of feelings. (For *The Melodious Chirping of the Fish Hawks*, see *Shi San Jing Zhu Shu*, p. 273.)

3.21 When Duke Ai asked Zai Wo[1] about the wooden tablet[2] for the God of Earth,[3] Zai Wo replied: "The Xia emperor[4] used pine; the Yin sovereign[5] used cypress; the Zhou sovereign[6] used chestnut, meant to make the people tremble."[7]

The Master, on hearing this, said: "What has been done, do not justify; what is irrevocable, do not dispute; what is past, do not censure."[8]

> 1. Alias of Zai Yu, one of Master Kong's major disciples.
> 2. A piece of narrow, elongated wood on which the name of the god or deceased ancestor it is supposed to represent is carved or written and to which the god or the spirit of the ancestor in question is believed to be attached, serving as an object of worship and sacrifice. To this day, such tablets can still be found in the ancestral temples of rural China.
> 3. One of the two most widely worshipped gods in ancient China, the other being the God of Grains. Their popularity may be ascribed to the fact that both earth and grains were vital to the subsistance of the people.

4. Referring to Xia Yu, the founding father of the Xia Dynasty.

5. Referring to Shang Tang, the founding father of the Shang Dynasty.

6. Referring to King Wu, the founding father of the Zhou Dynasty.

7. When a prince was granted a fief by the emperor to establish a state of his own, he was supposed to erect an altar to the God of Earth first and plant around it trees of a kind that suited its soil, and the wooden tablet for the God of Earth was supposed to be made with the wood of that particular kind of tree.

The character for "chestnut tree" (*li*) also means "to tremble" in classical Chinese.

8. The Master, who was out of the state at the time, heard about this episode and admonished his disciples against commenting on the faults of former rulers, which was a violation of the rituals.

3.22 The Master said: "Guan Zhong's[1] capacity was small indeed!"[2]

Someone said: "Guan Zhong was frugal, was he not?"

The Master said: "Guan Shi had three households, and his house officers[3] performed no additional duties other than their own. How could he be considered frugal?"

"However, Guan Zhong knew the rituals, did he not?"

The Master said: "The prince of the state had a screen wall[4] erected; Guan Shi, too, had a screen wall erected. The prince of the state, in promoting amity with another, had an earthen stand for returning drinking vessels; Guan Shi, too, had an earthen stand for returning drinking vessels. If Guan Shi knew the rituals, who does not know the rituals?"

1. Guan Zhong (?-645 B.C.E.), prime minister to Duke Huan of Qi, one of the worthiest statesmen in the Spring and Autumn period.

2. His contributions to the State of Qi as well as to the empire were prodigious (see 14.16, 14.17), but his moral accomplishments were deficient, as may be seen in this chapter; hence the Master's comment.

3. Lords and ministers also had officers to govern their fiefs for them and to counsel them on court affairs as well as the affairs of their respective noble houses. However, they were supposed to discharge miscellaneous duties in addition to the specific one assigned to them.

4. A privacy measure to shield those in the palace from the outside world.

3.23 The Master spoke to the Senior Music Master of Lu on musical performance, saying: "Musical performance is easy to understand: When it begins, it rises in stirring concert; when it goes into full swing, it is pure, distinct, and continuous until the finale."[1]

1. The Master was discussing the sequence of a performance of classical music of the day: first, a hymn sung to the accompaniment of big and small bells, which was sonorous and stirring; this was followed by the singing of the Ascension Song, which was pure; then a performance of the *sheng* (a reed pipe wind instrument), which was distinct; then the Alternation Song, in which singing alternated with performance of the *sheng* continuously until the finale, a grand ensemble of voice and instruments.

3.24 The frontier warden[1] of Yi County[2] requested an interview, saying: "Of all the gentlemen that visited this place, none has denied me an interview." Whereupon, the followers ushered him in.

On coming out, he said: "Gentlemen, why worry about the loss?[3] Long indeed has the empire lost the Way! Heaven shall use the Master as a wooden bell."[4]

1. One of the minor officers who kept watch at outposts on the borders of the empire or a state. The warden in this incident is generally believed by commentators to be a worthy man concealing himself in a low position.
2. A county of the State of Wei.
3. The Master's loss of office in Lu.
4. A bronze bell with a wooden tongue, used to rouse and assemble the multitudes when the emperor had a decree to proclaim or saw a need to edify the people; a metaphor signifying a great teacher of the people.

3.25 The Master said of *The Succession*: "Exceedingly beautiful! And exceedingly good!" He said of *Military Exploits*: "Exceedingly beautiful! But not exceedingly good."[1]

1. Master Kong considered *The Succession*, a piece of dance music in praise of the ancient sage king Shun, exceedingly beautiful and exceedingly good because Shun's throne was yielded to him voluntarily by the sage king Yao due to his great worth and sagacity. He considered *Military Exploits*, a piece of dance music in praise of King Wu of Zhou, exceedingly beautiful, but not exceedingly good, because King Wu obtained his throne through warfare.

3.26 The Master said: "Seated on high, he is not lenient; performing the rituals, he is not reverent; confronting mourning, he is not grief-stricken—How can I bear to look at all this!"[1]

1. This is said in regard to an inhumane ruler.

Book Four

LI REN (*To Live among Men of Humanity*)

4.1 The Master said: "To live among humane men is beautiful. Not to reside among humane men—how can one be considered wise?"[1]

> 1. My rendition is based on an ancient text of this chapter quoted in a note to the Han poet Zhang Heng's poem *Meditation on the Profundities of Life* (see Cheng Shu-de, *Lun Yu Ji Shi*, or *Collected Interpretations on Lun Yu*; Beijing: Zhonghua Press, 1990, p. 226).

4.2 The Master said: "An inhumane man cannot long abide in privation,[1] nor can he long abide in comfort.[2] A humane man is at ease with humanity;[3] a wise man benefits from humanity."[4]

> 1. He will commit theft or robbery. (Cf. 15.2.)
> 2. He will become extravagant and wanton.
> 3. One who is humane by nature practices humanity spontaneously; it comes natural to him.
> 4. A wise man, seeing the good of humanity, practices it to seek its benefit.

4.3 The Master said: "Only a humane man is capable of loving men, and capable of loathing men."[1]

> 1. He loves good men and loathes evil men. His likes and dislikes conform to righteousness. Only a humane man is capable of this.

4.4 The Master said: "If you bend your mind on humanity, you are free from evil."

4.5 The Master said: "Wealth and rank are what men desire: If you come by them undeservingly, you should not abide in them. Poverty and lowliness are what men loathe: If you come by them undeservingly,[1] you should not abandon them.[2] If a gentleman abandons humanity, how can he fulfill that name? A gentleman will not, for the space of a meal, depart from humanity. In haste and flurry, he always adheres to it; in fall and stumble, he always adheres to it."

1. That is, if you become poor through practicing humanity and righteousness.

2. This is in keeping with the Master's teaching that a gentleman should rest at ease in poverty and delight in the Way. (Cf. 6.11, 7.15, 15.2.)

4.6   The Master said: "I have never seen anyone who loves humanity, nor one who loathes inhumanity. One who loves humanity places nothing above it; one who loathes inhumanity, in practicing humanity, never allows anyone inhumane to affect his person. Is there anyone who can, for a single day, exert his energy on humanity? I have never seen any whose ability is insufficient. There may be such people; only I have not seen any."

4.7   The Master said: "People's faults may be ascribed to their respective kind.[1] In observing faults, you get to know the man."[2]

1. For instance, a humane man often errs in being overly compassionate and tolerating vices; an inhumane man often errs in being callous and cruel.

2. That is, whether he is humane or not.

4.8   The Master said: "If, in the morning, I should hear about the Way, in the evening, I would die contented!"[1]

1. The Master was deploring that he would never hear about the sage kings' Way prevailing in the world again.

A variant reading says: "If, in the morning, one hears the Way, in the evening, one may die contented."

4.9   The Master said: "A *shi*[1] who aspires after the Way but is ashamed of poor clothes and poor food is not worth discoursing with."

1. That class of men who ranked between ministers and commoners, inclusive of minor officials and scholars.

4.10   The Master said: "The gentleman, in his attitude toward all under heaven, neither favors anyone nor disfavors anyone. He keeps close to whoever is righteous."

4.11   The Master said: "The gentleman cherishes virtue; the small man cherishes land. The gentleman cherishes institutions; the small man cherishes favors."[1]

1. What the gentleman concerns himself about most is his moral accomplishments; what the small man concerns himself about most is his personal interests. "Institutions" here refers to ritual institutions.

4.12 The Master said: "Acting solely in pursuit of profit will incur much resentment."

4.13 The Master said: "If you can govern a state with courtesy and deference, what difficulty do you have in conducting state affairs?[1] If you cannot govern a state with courtesy and deference, what can you do with the rituals?"[2]

1. Surviving texts of *Lun Yu* lack the words "in conducting state affairs" (*Yu cong zheng hu*). This reconstruction makes better sense and also makes the sentence more balanced in structure.
2. Then, there will be a lot of contention and chaos, and the rituals will be useless to the ruler.

4.14 The Master said: "Do not worry about having no office; rather, worry about whether you deserve to stand in that office. Do not worry about nobody knowing you; rather, seek to be worth knowing."[1]

1. Cf. 1.16, 14.30, 15.19.

4.15 The Master said: "Well, Shen,[1] my Way is threaded together in one string."
Master Zeng said: "Right."
When the Master went out, the pupils[2] asked: "What did he mean?"
Master Zeng said: "The Master's Way consists in wholehearted sincerity and like-hearted considerateness,[3] that is all."

1. The disciple Zeng Shen.
2. Master Zeng's students.
3. Cf. 5.12, 6.30, 12.2, 15.3, 15.24.

4.16 The Master said: "The gentleman is conversant with righteousness; the small man is conversant with profit."[1]

1. "The gentleman" and "the small man" here are distinguished by virtue rather than by rank.

4.17 The Master said: "On seeing a worthy man, think of equaling him; on seeing an unworthy man, examine yourself inwardly."[1]

  1. Cf. 16.11.

4.18 The Master said: "In serving your parents, be gentle in remonstration.[1] Seeing that they are not inclined to comply, remain reverent, and do not disobey them. Though weary, do not feel resentful."

  1. I.e., when they do something wrong.

4.19 The Master said: "When your parents are alive, do not travel far. If you do travel, be sure to have a regular destination."[1]

  1. So that they may feel at ease and will be able to summon you back in the event of an emergency.

4.20 The Master said: "If, for three years, a man does not change his father's Way, he may be said to be filial."[1]

  1. Cf. 1.11.

4.21 The Master said: "Your parents' age you must bear in mind: on the one hand, with joy; on the other, with anxiety."[1]

  1. You are happy to see them enjoying a long life, but apprehensive because they are getting older and weaker.

4.22 The Master said: "The reason that the ancients would not rashly utter words is that they deemed it shameful not to live up to them."[1]

  1. Cf. 1.14, 2.13, 4.24, 12.3, 14.20, 14.27. Note that the word "wang" (rashly) is only found in He Yan's ancient text.

4.23 The Master said: "Those who err through self-restraint are rare indeed."

4.24 The Master said: "The gentleman wishes to be slow in speech but brisk in action."[1]

  1. Cf. 1.14, 2.13, 4.22, 12.3, 14.20, 14.27.

4.25 The Master said: "The virtuous are not solitary. They surely have neighbors."

4.26 Zi-you said: "Serving the sovereign intimately brings humiliation; associating with friends with intimately brings alienation."[1]

1. Compare the Confucian proverb on friendship: "The gentleman's friendship is as bland as water; the small man's friendship is as sweet as nectar."

Book Five

GONG-YE CHANG

5.1 The Master said of Gong-ye Chang:[1] "He deserves to be wived. Although once bound in black ropes,[2] he was not guilty of the crime." So he gave his daughter to him in marriage.

> 1. One of Master Kong's major disciples.
> 2. In ancient times, criminals were bound in black ropes. Chang was imprisoned for a crime he had not committed.

5.2 The Master said of Nan Rong:[1] "When the state possessed the Way, he was not cast out of office; when the state lost the Way,[2] he was exempt from punishment and slaying." So he gave his elder brother's daughter to him in marriage.

> 1. Alias of Nan-gong Kuo, one of Master Kong's major disciples.
> 2. "To possess the Way" here means "to be well ruled" and "to lose the Way," "to be ill ruled."

5.3 The Master said of Zi-jian:[1] "What a gentleman that man is! However, if there were no gentlemen in Lu, where could he have acquired all that?"[2]

> 1. Alias of Fu Bi-qi, one of Master Kong's major disciples.
> 2. His moral accomplishments.

5.4 Zi-gong asked: "What do you think of me?"
The Master said: "You are a utensil."[1]
Zi-gong said: "What utensil?"
The Master said: "A *hu* or a *lian*."[2]

> 1. See 2.12, note 1.
> 2. Names of valuable sacrificial vessels, a metaphor representing a man of unusual capacity.

5.5 Someone said: "Yong[1] is humane but not eloquent."

The Master said: "What does he need eloquence for? To confront people with a glib tongue often makes them detest you. I do not know[2] about his being humane, but what does he need eloquence for?"

1. Ran Yong, one of Master Kong's major disciples.

2. "I do not know" was the Master's mild way of showing negation or modesty.

5.6 When the Master asked Qi-diao Kai[1] to take office, the latter replied: "Of that I am not very confident yet."

The Master was pleased.[2]

1. One of Master Kong's major disciples.

2. The Master was pleased that Kai was so humble and devoted to learning.

5.7 The Master said: "If the Way should fail to prevail, I would board a raft and float to sea.[1] The one to follow me would probably be Iou."

Zi-lu, on hearing this, was pleased.

The Master said: "Iou is braver than I, but that is not something to recommend him."[2]

1. Some commentators believe that the Master had Korea in mind when he made this remark.

2. Two variant readings of this remark are: "However, there is nowhere to acquire the lumber [meant to be a humorous remark]" and

"Only he does not know how to weigh matters and make judgments."

5.8 Meng Wu-bo[1] asked: "Is Zi-lu humane?"

The Master said: "I do not know."

When he asked again, the Master said: "Iou is one who, in a thousand-chariot state, may be engaged to command its army. I do not know about his being humane."

"What about Qiu?"[2]

The Master said: "Qiu is one who, in a thousand-household county or a hundred-chariot fief, may be engaged to be its magistrate. I do not know about his being humane."

"What about Chi?"[3]

The Master said: "Chi is one who, standing in court with a

fastened sash,[4] may be engaged to converse with guests of state.[5] I do not know about his being humane."

1. See 2.6, note 1.
2. Given name of the disciple Ran You.
3. Gong-xi Chi, one of Master Kong's major disciples.
4. I.e., in official attire. An official robe was supposed to be fastened with a sash.
5. I.e., to discharge diplomatic duties.

5.9   The Master said to Zi-gong: "Between you and Hui, which is superior?"

Zi-gong replied: "How dare I compare with Hui? Hui hears one thing and thereby knows ten. I hear one thing and thereby know two."

The Master said: "You are not his equal. I agree with you: You are not his equal."[1]

1. A variant reading of this sentence is: "You and I are not his equals."

5.10   Zai Yu slept during the day. The Master said: "Rotten wood is beyond carving; a dung-and-mud wall is beyond plastering. As for Yu, what is the use of reprimanding him?"

The Master said:[1] "At first, my attitude toward men was to hear their words and believe in their deeds. Now my attitude toward men is to hear their words and observe their deeds. It was due to Yu that I have changed this."

1. What follows might have been said on another occasion.

5.11   The Master said: "I have never seen a staunch man."[1]

Someone said: "There is Shen Cheng."[2]

The Master said: "Cheng is lustful. How could he be staunch?"

1. One who is firmly committed to the pursuit of the Way and will not change his course under whatever pressure.
2. One of Master Kong's major disciples.

5.12   Zi-gong said: "What I do not wish others to impose on me, I also do not wish to impose on others."[1]

The Master said: "Ci, this is beyond your reach."[2]

1. This is like-hearted considerateness, which is equivalent to humanity. (Cf. 4.15, 6.30, 12.2, 15.24.)

2. Humanity stems from innate goodness, for the most part endowed by nature, and cannot be acquired merely through postnatal effort. Hence the Master's comment.

5.13 Zi-gong said: "The Master's cultural accomplishments—we get to hear them, but the Master's ideas on human nature and the Way of Heaven[1]—we hardly get to hear them."[2]

1. In *Lun Yu*, the Way of Heaven (or the decree of Heaven) generally governs such matters as life and death, wealth and rank, good fortune and misfortune, success and failure, etc. (Cf. 12.5.)

2. The reason for this is that the Master instructed solely on the duties of man and rarely discussed matters bordering on the unknown. (Cf. 6.22, 7.20, 9.1.)

5.14 When Zi-lu heard something and had not been able to practice it as yet, he was apprehensive that he might hear something else.[1]

1. This chapter portrays Zi-lu as someone who earnestly practiced what he had learnt.

5.15 Zi-gong asked: "Why was Kong Wen-zi[1] called 'Wen'?"
The Master said: "Intelligent and fond of learning, not ashamed to consult his inferiors—that is why he was called 'Wen.'"

1. Minister of Wei; *Wen*, which was his posthumous title, means "refined."

5.16 The Master said of Zi-chan:[1] "He possessed four virtues of the gentleman's Way: he conducted himself respectfully; he served the sovereign reverently; he provided for the people beneficently; he employed the people reasonably."

1. Zi-chan (?-522 B.C.E), prime minister of Zheng, one of the worthiest statesmen of the period, much admired by Master Kong. When he died, the Master wept and said: "He was beloved by the people like one of the ancients."

5.17 The Master said: "Yan Ping-zhong[1] was good at making friends. Years later, he still revered them."[2]

1. Prime minister of Qi, a worthy statesman of the period, much admired by the Master.

2. A variant reading is: "Years later, his friends still revered him."

5.18   The Master said: "Zang Wen-zhong[1] housed a Cai[2] in a hall with hills carved on the brackets of its capitals and aquatic plants painted on the columns of its beams. What do you think of his wisdom?"[3]

1. Minister of Lu. (Cf. 15.14.)

2. Name of a species of tortoise, which came from the State of Cai, near the present-day Shang-cai, Anhui Province, and was used exclusively by the emperor for divination. Zang's keeping one for himself was an act of usurpation.

3. Zang was generally known as a wise man; hence the Master's sarcasm.

5.19   Zi-zhang asked: "Prime Minister Zi-wen[1] was thrice[2] appointed prime minister and never showed any sign of joy. He was thrice dismissed and never showed any sign of resentment. The old prime minister's[3] government decrees he always imparted to the new prime minister. What do you think of him?"

The Master said: "Loyal indeed."

Zi-zhang said: "Was he humane?"

The Master said: "I do not know. But how could he be considered humane?"

"The viscount of Cui[4] having assassinated the prince of Qi[5], Chen Wen-zi,[6] who possessed ten teams of horses,[7] abandoned them and left the state. On arriving in another, he said: 'They are just like our minister the viscount of Cui.' Having left that state and arriving in a third, he again said: 'They are just like our minister the Viscount of Cui.' And again left it. What do you think of him?"

The Master said: "Pure indeed."

Zi-zhang said: "Was he humane?"

The Master said: "I do not know. But how could he be considered humane?"

1. Prime minister of Chu, one of the worthy statesmen of the period, much admired by the Master.

2. "Thrice" in classical Chinese often means "several times."

3. Zi-wen himself.

4. Cui Zhu, minister of Qi.

5. Duke Zhuang of Qi.

6. Minister of Qi.

7. Each team was made of 4 horses, hence a total of 40 horses.

5.20 Ji Wen-zi[1] contemplated thrice before acting. The Master, on hearing this, said: "Twice was enough."

1. Minister of Lu, *Wen* being his posthumous title, prime minister of Lu before the Master's day. Loyal and prudent, he made few mistakes in government. Hence, the Master's commendatory remark.

5.21 The Master said: "Ning Wu-zi[1]—when the state possessed the Way, he was wise; when the state lost the Way, he was stupid.[2] His wisdom can be emulated, but his stupidity cannot be emulated."

1. Minister of Wei.

2. When the sovereign was tyrannical or fatuous, he would conceal his talents by feigning stupidity.

5.22 The Master, when in Chen,[1] said: "Let us go home! Let us go home! Our young people at home are high-minded, simple, and endowed with brilliant talents. I do not know how to cut them."[2]

1. A small state of the period, in the present-day Huai-yang, Henan Province.

2. The metaphor is to cut a piece of fabric into the shape of a garment. The Master was anxious to go home and instruct the young people at home in the Way of humanity.

A variant reading of this remark is: "Only they do not know how to weigh matters and make judgments."

5.23 The Master said: "Bo-yi and Shu-qi[1] never bore old grudges; resentment was therefore little."[2]

1. Two ancients of the Yin Dynasty whom the Master admired greatly and commended as men of humanity. (See 7.14, note 2.)

2. People's resentment against them.

5.24 The Master said: "Who said Wei-sheng Gao[1] was straightforward? When someone begged some vinegar of him, he begged some of his neighbor and gave it to the man."

1. Native of Lu, known as a straightforward man.

5.25 The Master said: "Sweet words, a pleasing countenance,[1] and excessive respectfulness—Zuo-qiu Ming[2] deems it shameful; I also deem it shameful. To conceal one's resentment against a person and befriend him—Zuo-qiu Ming deems it shameful; I also deem it shameful."

1. Cf. 1.3, 17.16.
2. Allegedly one of Master Kong's disciples, also one of the three commentators of *The Spring and Autumn Annals*, a history of the state of Lu.

5.26 When Yan Yuan and Ji-lu[1] were in attendance, the Master said: "Why do you not each speak your aspirations?"

Zi-lu said: "I wish to share my carriage, horses, clothes, and furs with my friends and wear them out without regret."

Yan Yuan said: "I wish never to brag about my merits, nor to parade my achievements."

Zi-lu said: "We should like to hear your aspirations, sir."

The Master said: "I wish to comfort the old, be truthful to friends, and cherish the young."[2]

1. Another alias of Zi-lu.
2. A variant reading of this quotation is: "I wish to make the old content with me, friends trust me, and the young cherish my memory."

5.27 The Master said: "Oh, it is all over! I have never seen anyone who can, on seeing his own fault, inwardly reprove himself."

5.28 The Master said: "Even a ten-household hamlet must have wholeheartedly sincere and truthful people like me, maybe not as fond of learning as I am."

Book Six

YONG YE *(Yong)*

6.1 The Master said: "Yong[1] could be made to sit facing due south."[2]

> 1. Ran Yong, or Ran Bo-niu, was one of the four disciples who excelled in moral conduct at Master Kong's school. (See 11.3.)
> 2. I.e., to rule as the reigning prince of a state. Note that in ancient China, a sovereign was supposed to sit in court with his face toward the south where the sky light came in. To this day, as a rule, Chinese houses have their doors open to the south.

6.2 When Zhong-gong asked about Zi-sang Bo-zi,[1] the Master said: "He is commendable for being simple."

Zhong-gong said: "To conduct himself with reverence and discharge his duties with simplicity in presiding over the people is commendable, is it not? However, to conduct himself with simplicity and discharge his duties with simplicity, is it not overly simple?"[2]

The Master said: "Yong, your remarks are correct."

> 1. Native of Lu. Not much is known about this man.
> 2. Zhong-gong was saying that to discharge one's duties in simple ways makes it easy and convenient for the people, which is good; but by conducting oneself with simplicity and discharging one's duties in simple ways, one tends to be negligent in self-cultivation and to lose one's dignity as well as the people's respect, which is not good.

6.3 Duke Ai asked: "Which of your disciples loves learning?"

Master Kong replied: "There was one Yan Hui, who loved learning. He never raised his anger or repeated a mistake. Unfortunately, he died young. Now there is none. I have not heard of any who loves learning."

6.4 When Zi-hua[1] was dispatched as an envoy to Qi, Master Ran,[2] on behalf of his mother, requested some millet.

The Master said: "Give her a *fu*."[3]

When requested to add some, the Master said: "Give her a *yu*."[4] Master Ran gave her five *bing*[5] of millet.

The Master said: "When Chi departed for Qi, he rode a fat horse and wore a soft fur robe. I hear it: 'The gentleman relieves the hard-pressed; he does not add to the rich.' "

1. Alias of Gong-xi Chi, one of Master Kong's major disciples.

2. Referring to Ran Qiu. That Ran Qiu was addressed as "Master" here shows that this chapter was most likely recorded by one of his pupils. Master Kong and Ran Qiu were both in office in Lu during this period.

3. An ancient Chinese dry measure unit equivalent to about 32 liters.

4. Approximately 12 liters.

5. 5 *bing* is approximately 4,000 liters, almost a hundred times what Master Kong had intended to give her.

6.5 When Yuan Si[1] served as his magistrate,[2] the Master gave him nine hundred[3] millet. Yuan Si declined.

The Master said: "Don't! Give some to your neighbors and countrymen."

1. Alias of Yuan Xian, one of Master Kong's major disciples.

2. When Master Kong was minister of justice in Lu, he employed Yuan Si as the magistrate of his fief.

3. The measurement unit is missing in the text. It is generally believed to be 900 *dou*, equivalent to 9,000 liters. Note that salaries were paid in grain in ancient China. This was probably Yuan Si's annual salary.

6.6 The Master, speaking about Zhong-gong, said: "A plough-ox's[1] calf, with red hide and well-shaped horns[2]—even though men might not want to use it,[3] would the mountains and rivers[4] abandon it?"

1. A plough-ox was considered unfit for sacrifice.

2. Both qualities were considered desirable for sacrificial purposes.

3. Zhong-gong might have been rejected from office at this time due to his father's low station in life.

4. I.e., the gods of mountains and rivers.

6.7 The Master said: "Hui is one whose heart, for three moons on end,[1] does not depart from humanity. The rest can only reach this once a day or once a moon, that is all."

1. I.e., for a long time.

6.8 Ji Kang-zi asked: "Can Zhong Iou[1] be engaged to conduct state affairs?"

The Master said: "Iou is resolute. In conducting state affairs, what difficulty does he have?"

Ji Kang-zi said: "Can Ci[2] be engaged to conduct state affairs?"

The Master said: "Ci is perceptive. In conducting state affairs, what difficulty does he have?"

Ji Kang-zi said: "Can Qiu[3] be engaged to conduct state affairs?"

The Master said: "Qiu is versatile. In conducting state affairs, what difficulty does he have?"

1. Full name of the disciple Zi-lu.
2. Given name of the disciple Zi-gong.
3. Given name of the disciple Ran You.

6.9 When Ji Shi[1] sent for Min Zi-qian[2] to serve as magistrate of Bi,[3] Min Zi-qian said: "Tactfully apologize for me.[4] If he sends for me again, I will surely be north of River Wen."[5]

1. Ji Kang-zi, then prime minister of Lu.
2. Alias of Min Shun, one of Master Kong's prominent disciples.
3. Bi County, Ji Shi's fief, situated to the northwest of the present-day Bi County, Shangdong Province.
4. A variant reading of this remark is: "Kindly decline for me."
5. The present-day Da-wen River in Shangdong Province. "I will surely be north of River Wen" means "I must escape to the State of Qi [which was north of River Wen]."

6.10 When Bo-niu[1] was sick, the Master went to inquire after his disease and held his hand from outside the window.[2]

The Master said: "We shall lose him. It is fated! Oh, that such a man should have contracted such a disease! Oh, that such a man should have contracted such a disease!"

1. Alias of Ran Geng, one of Master Kong's major disciples.
2. Having contracted a foul disease, possibly leprosy, Bo-niu did not wish to see visitors.

6.11 The Master said: "How worthy Hui is! Eating out of a bamboo container, drinking out of a gourd ladle, and living in a narrow shack¹—others would be utterly dejected, but Hui never alters his delight. How worthy Hui is!"

1. A variant reading of this passage is: "Having only a bamboo-containerful of rice and a ladleful of water and living in a narrow alley . . ."

6.12   Ran Qiu said: "Not that I do not like your Way, sir, but that my ability is insufficient."

The Master said: "Those whose ability is insufficient give up halfway. Now you have drawn a halting line."

6.13   The Master said to Zi-xia: "You be a gentleman *ru*,¹ and not a small-man *ru*."

1. The word *ru* in Master Kong's day referred to a scholar-teacher (*shiru*). At this juncture, Zi-xia had started a school of his own; hence the Master's admonition. (For *ru*, see Terms, p. 34.)

6.14   When Zi-you served as Magistrate of Wu City,¹ the Master said: "Have you found any men?"²

Zi-you said: "There is one Dan-tai Mie-ming,³ who, when walking, never takes a short cut and, except on official business, never comes to my house."

1. A county of Lu, situated to the southwest of what is now Bi County, Shandong Province.
2. Worthy men fit to serve as officials.
3. Later to be one of Master Kong's major disciples.

6.15   The Master said: "Meng Zhi-fan¹ never brags. In a rout, he brought up the rear.² About to enter the city gate, he whipped his horse, saying: 'Not that I dared to bring up the rear, but that my horse refused to make headway.'"³

1. Minister of Lu. Not much is known about this man.
2. It was considered a valiant act to bring up the rear in a retreat.
3. This episode is recorded in *Chun Qiu Zuo Zhuan* (*Zuo's Commentary on The Spring and Autumn Annals*), *Duke Ai*, 11th year. (See *Shi San Jing Zhu Shu*, p. 2166.)

6.16   The Master said: "He who possesses neither Zhu Tuo's[1] eloquence nor Song Chao's[2] good looks[3] will find it difficult to be immune from the perils of today's world."[4]

> 1. Minister of Wei, noted for his eloquence. (See 14.19.)
> 2. A nobleman from the State of Song, Chao being his name; minister of Wei.
> 3. A variant reading of this clause is: "If you do not possess Zhu Tuo's eloquence but instead possess Song Chao's good looks, . . ."
> 4. The Master deplored the decadence of the period in which eloquence and good looks were valued above loyalty and uprightness.

6.17   The Master said: "Who can go out without passing through the doorway? How is it that no one will follow this Way?"

6.18   The Master said: "When simplicity[1] surpasses refinement,[2] one is a rustic;[3] when refinement surpasses simplicity, one is a scribe.[4] Only when refinement and simplicity are well blended can one become a gentleman."[5]

> 1. I.e., native goodness of heart.
> 2. I.e., the acquisition and application of the rituals.
> 3. A metaphor representing a man who possesses native goodness of heart but little accomplishment in the rituals.
> 4. An auxiliary functionary in charge of official documents, a metaphor representing a man conversant with the formalities of the rituals but deficient in native goodness of heart.
> 5. This chapter discusses the constant mean between simplicity and refinement in the composition of a gentleman.

6.19   The Master said: "That man lives owes to uprightness; that a crooked man lives with impunity owes to sheer luck."

6.20   The Master said: "Those who know it[1] are not comparable to those who love it; those who love it are not comparable to those who delight in it."

> 1. The Way.

6.21   The Master said: "To people above average, one can impart higher things; to people below average, one cannot impart higher things."[1]

> 1. This chapter deals with the Master's methodology of teaching in accordance with the learner's aptitude.

6.22   When Fan Chi asked about wisdom, the Master said: "To apply oneself to the duties of man[1] and, while revering the spirits and gods, to keep away from them—this may be called wisdom."

   When he asked about humanity, the Master said: "A man of humanity places hard work before reward.[2] This may be called humanity."

   1. The ten duties of man are: the father's lovingness, the son's filial piety, the elder brother's kindness, the younger brother's obedience, the husband's dutifulness, the wife's compliance, the senior's beneficence, the junior's submissiveness, the sovereign's humaneness, and the subject's loyalty.
   2. A variant reading of this quotation is: "Humanity means going forward in hard work and staying behind in taking reward." (Cf. 12.21, 15.38.)

6.23   The Master said: "The man of wisdom delights in water;[1] the man of humanity delights in mountains.[2] The man of wisdom is active;[3] the man of humanity is still.[4] The man of wisdom is happy;[5] the man of humanity is long-lived."[6]

   1. He delights in exercising his talents to achieve good government, like water flowing incessantly.
   2. He delights in staying peaceful and firm like a mountain that, sitting motionless, allows the ten thousand things to grow exuberantly.
   3. He keeps progressing everyday, hence he is active.
   4. He is free from lust, hence he is still.
   5. He exerts himself and achieves his purpose, hence he is happy.
   6. He is by nature tranquil, hence he is long-lived.

6.24   The Master said: "Qi, once transformed, would reach the state of Lu; Lu, once transformed, would reach the Way."[1]

   1. The states of Qi and Lu were still under the good influence of their founding fathers, the Grand Duke and Duke Dan of Zhou, respectively, the former being an eminently worthy man and the latter a sage. Having preserved the rituals instituted by Duke Dan, Lu was superior to Qi in government and culture. If there should emerge wise princes to revitalize these states, Qi could be made to reach the state of Lu, and Lu could be transformed into a state where the sage kings' Way prevailed.

6.25   The Master said: "A *gu*[1] is no longer a *gu*! Is this a *gu*? Is this a *gu*?"[2]

1. A drinking vessel, round at the top and square at the bottom, with ridges on all sides, used at the Prefecture Magistrate's Drinking Ceremony. People at the time defied the traditional pattern of the *gu* as prescribed by the rituals. Hence the Master's disapproval.

2. The Master deplored that his contemporaries only indulged themselves in drinking but had no regard for the rituals.

6.26 Zai Wo asked: "A humane man—if someone should tell him that there is a man in the well, would he follow him into it?"

The Master said: "Why should he do so? The gentleman might be made to rush over but could not be made to jump in. He might be deceived but could not be duped."

6.27 The Master said: "A gentleman who is extensively learned in culture[1] and restrains himself with the rituals is not likely to betray."[2]

1. I.e., the classics.
2. To betray the Way.

6.28 When the Master had an audience with Nan-zi,[1] Zi-lu was displeased. The Master, swearing to him, said: "If I have done anything improper, may Heaven forsake me! May Heaven forsake me!"

1. Wife to Duke Ling of Wei, notoriously promiscuous but influential in state affairs. When she summoned Master Kong for an audience, he was obliged by the rituals to comply.

6.29 The Master said: "The constant mean[1] as a virtue is sublime indeed! The people have been unable to practice it for a long time!"

1. See section on Terms, p. 24.

6.30 Zi-gong said: "If there is someone who can give extensively to the people and relieve the multitudes, what do you think of him? Can he be called a man of humanity?"

The Master said: "Far more than a man of humanity. He must be a sage! Even Yao[1] and Shun[2] found it difficult. For a man of humanity is one who, wishing to establish himself,[3] helps others to establish themselves and who, wishing to gain perception,[4] helps others to gain perception. He is able to take himself as an example.[5] This may be called the approach to humanity."

1. One of the legendary sage kings admired most by the Master. By employing Shun as his regent, he achieved humane government. Because his son Dan-zhu was unworthy, Yao eventually abdicated and ceded the throne to Shun.

2. Another of the legendary sage kings admired most by the Master. By employing such worthy men as Yu and Gao Yao, he achieved humane government, too. As his son Shang-jun was also unworthy, he eventually abdicated and ceded the throne to his minister Yu, who had tamed the Yellow River for him.

3. I.e., to stand firmly on the rituals.

4. I.e., to acquire a thorough understanding of the Way of humanity.

5. The Master was discoursing on the doctrine of wholehearted sincerity and like-hearted considerateness, the approach to humanity. (Cf. 4.15, 5.12, 12.2, 15.24.)

Book Seven

SHU ER *(I Transmit and)*

7.1 The Master said: "I transmit and do not create.[1] I believe in and love antiquity, secretly comparing myself to our Lao Peng."[2]

> 1. That is, I pass on the Six Classics and do not introduce new rituals and music.
>
> 2. This man's identity is controversial; possibly he was a worthy minister of the Yin Dynasty who delighted in transmitting the wisdom of the ancients.

7.2 The Master said: "To memorize silently, learn insatiably, and instruct others indefatigably—what difficulty do they present to me?"

7.3 The Master said: "Virtue uncultivated, learning undiscussed, the inability to move toward righteousness after hearing it, and the inability to correct my imperfections—these are my anxieties."

7.4 When the Master was at leisure, he looked tidy and relaxed.

7.5 The Master said: "How utterly I have declined! Long indeed since I last dreamt of seeing Duke of Zhou."[1]

> 1. Title of Ji Dan (?–1104? B.C.E.), one of the sages most admired by the Master, son to King Wen, younger brother to King Wu, and uncle Regent to King Cheng of Zhou, founding father of the State of Lu. He helped to establish the rituals and institutions in the early stages of the Zhou Dynasty.

7.6 The Master said: "Aspire after the Way; adhere to virtue; rely on humanity; ramble among the arts."[1]

> 1. Referring to the Six Arts, namely, the rituals, music, archery, charioteering, language, and arithmetic.

7.7 The Master said: "To anyone who spontaneously came to me with a bundle of dried pork,[1] I have never denied instruction."

1. Ten strips of dried pork, considered the most insignificant gift on one's first visit to a person. (Cf. 15.39.)

7.8 The Master said: "No vexation, no enlightenment; no anxiety, no illumination.¹ If I have brought up one corner and he does not return with the other three,² I will not repeat."

1. The Master urged his disciples to take the initiative in learning: they should be eager and dedicated in learning.
2. When a student was taught something, he was expected to draw relevant inferences from it.

7.9 When the Master dined beside a bereaved person, he never ate his fill.

If the Master had wept on that day, he would not sing.

7.10 The Master said to Yan Yuan: "When employed, to put it¹ into practice; when unemployed, to keep it in store—perhaps only you and I are capable of this."

Zi-lu said: "Sir, if you were to command the three armies,² whom would you have with you?"

The Master said: "He who wrestles a tiger bare-handed, or crosses a river bare-footed and dies without regret—I would not have him. It must be someone who, confronting a task, is apprehensive and who is good not only at making stratagems but also implementing them."

1. The pronoun *zhi* (it) is generally understood to stand for "the Way" in both cases.
2. A large state was entitled to three armies, each comprising 12,500 men.

7.11 The Master said: "If wealth and rank could be sought,¹ be it a whip-holder's office,² I would take it. If it cannot be sought, I shall follow my liking."³

1. "Wealth and rank" implies a government office, for in those days the only way to acquire wealth was through a high official salary. What the Master really meant was that wealth and rank were predestined by the decree of Heaven and therefore could not be sought.
2. One of the lowest official positions.
3. That is, the Way of the sage kings. During this period of the Master's life, the three noble houses were in control of state power in Lu. Hence the

Master refrained from taking office and engaged himself in editing and transmitting the classics.

7.12 The things that the Master treated with discretion were: fasting,[1] war, and sickness.

> 1. The ancients fasted before a sacrificial ceremony to show reverence for the gods or their ancestors.

7.13 When the Master was in Qi, he heard *The Succession*.[1] For three moons, he could not tell the taste of pork,[2] saying: "I never imagined that learning music could come to this!"

> 1. See 3.25, note 1.
> 2. He was too immersed in studying the music of *The Succession*.

7.14 Ran You said: "Does the Master support the prince of Wei?"[1]
Zi-gong said: "All right. I shall ask him."
On entering, he said: "What kind of men were Bo-yi and Shu-qi?"[2]
The Master said: "Worthy men of antiquity."
Zi-gong said: "Did they have any regrets?"
The Master said: "They sought humanity and attained humanity. What regrets did they have?"
On coming out, Zi-gong said: "The Master does not support him."[3]

> 1. Duke Chu of Wei, grandson to Duke Ling and son to Crown Prince Kuai-kui. He seized the throne while his father was in exile.
> 2. Sons of the prince of the State of Gu-zhu toward the end of the Yin Dynasty. When their father died, each fled the country to yield the throne to the other; both ended in starvation.
> 3. The story of Bo-yi and Shu-qi formed a sharp contrast to that of Duke Chu and his father Kuai-kui, who contended for the throne. On hearing the Master praise Bo-yi and Shu-qi, Zi-gong immediately realized that he did not approve of the duke's appropriation of his father's throne.
> Zi-gong asked the question in such a roundabout way because he knew it was against the rituals for the Master to openly censure the duke who was his host.

7.15 The Master said: "Eating coarse food, drinking plain water, and bending one arm for a pillow—happiness also lies therein. Wealth and rank acquired through unrighteous means are to me like drifting clouds."[1]

1. Cf. 1.14, 1.15, 4.9, 6.11.

7.16 The Master said: "Lend me a few years so that at fifty, I may learn *Changes*[1] and thereby be immune from gross errors."

1. *The Book of Changes*, one of the Five Classics edited and transmitted by Master Kong, an ancient book of divination replete with philosophical ideas. An exceedingly subtle text, it explores natural laws, human nature, and the decree of Heaven. The Master knew the decree of Heaven at fifty (2.4). So, to study the book that explores the decree of Heaven at an age when he realized the decree of Heaven, he hoped that he might be immune from gross errors. At this juncture, the Master was in his late forties.

7.17 The Master followed the standard pronunciation[1] in reciting poetry and history. In conducting the rituals, he invariably followed the standard pronunciation.[2]

1. I.e., the dialect of Hao-jing, the western capital of the Zhou Dynasty (southwest of what is now Chang-an, Shaanxi Province). Hence, the present-day Shaanxi dialect.
2. A variant reading of this chapter is: "The Master often discoursed on *Poetry, History*, and the conducting of rituals—these are the things he often discoursed on."

7.18 When the Duke of She[1] asked Zi-lu about Master Kong, Zi-lu did not reply.
The Master said: "Why did you not say: 'He is a man who, when absorbed,[2] forgets his meals; when enraptured,[3] forgets his anxiety, not even aware that old age is drawing near' and the like?"

1. Title of Shen Zhu-liang, a worthy minister of Chu, which was a large non-Chinese state to the South of the Yangtze River.
2. I.e., when absorbed in his studies.
3. I.e., when enraptured by the Way.

7.19 The Master said: "I am not one who knows it[1] at birth, but one who loves antiquity and assiduously seeks it."

1. The Way.

7.20 The Master would not discourse on mystery, force, rebellion, and deity.[1]

> 1. The Master discoursed on the constant and not the mysterious, virtue and not force, good government and not rebellion, the affairs of man and not those of the unknown.

7.21 The Master said: "When three men walk together,[1] I can surely find my teachers. I choose their merits to follow and their imperfections to correct."

> 1. Master Kong was one of them.

7.22 The Master said: "Since Heaven has endowed me with moral force, what can Huan Tui do to me?"[1]

> 1. During Master Kong's travels through the various states, he arrived in Song, where he practiced the rituals with his disciples under a big tree. Huan Tui, Song's minister of military affairs, eldest brother to the Master's disciple Sima Niu, who was intent on killing the Master, felled the tree—upon which the Master departed and made this remark when the disciples urged him to hurry up.

7.23 The Master said: "Gentlemen, do you think I am concealing things from you? I am not concealing anything from you. I do nothing without sharing it with you gentlemen. This is the kind of man I am."[1]

> 1. Master Kong seldom discoursed on human nature and the decree of Heaven. Hence the disciples' suspicion that he might be hiding things from them.

7.24 The Master instructed in four aspects: culture, moral conduct, wholehearted sincerity, and truthfulness.[1]

> 1. Wholehearted sincerity and truthfulness being the two basic virtues in the Way of humanity.

7.25 The Master said: "A sage man[1]—I shall never get to see one now. If I get to see a gentleman,[2] I shall be contented."

The Master said:[3] "A benevolent man[4]—I shall never get to see one now. If I get to see a man of constancy,[5] I shall be contented.

Those who have not but pretend to have, who are empty but pretend to be full, and who are hard up but pretend to be opulent are difficult to consider constant."[6]

1. I.e., a sage king.
2. I.e., a virtuous king.
3. Possibly on a later occasion.
4. I.e., a benevolent prince. (Cf. 11.19, 13.11, 13.29.)
5. I.e., a prince who adhered to moral principles faithfully.
6. Bragging and pretension were the vogue among the princes of the Master's day.

Note that "have not" and "have" are said in regard to the Way; "empty" and "full" are said in regard to virtue.

7.26 The Master fished with a hook, but not with a big rope;[1] he shot at flying birds, but not at roosting ones.[2]

1. This was an ancient fishing device. The big rope had silk strings hanging down from it, each with a hook fastened to its end. It was stretched across a stream to intercept fish and was able to bring in dozens at once, whereas fishing with a hook could catch only one fish at a time.
2. This chapter demonstrates the Master's compassion in hunting and fishing.

7.27 The Master said: "There are people who write without knowing anything about it.[1] I am not like that. I hear much and choose what is good to follow; I see much and memorize it.[2] I belong to the second category in acquiring it."[3]

1. "It" stands for the Way here, as is often the case in *Lun Yu*.
2. This clause should read: "I see much and choose what is good to memorize." The omission is to avoid redundancy.
3. That is, those who know it through learning, the first category being those who know it (the Way of humanity) at birth. (Cf. 16.9.)

7.28 When a lad from the Hu Prefecture[1] who had been difficult to talk to was given an interview, the disciples were perplexed.

The Master said: "I approve of his progress and do not approve of his retrogress. Why so harsh? When a person cleanses himself to come forward, I approve of his cleanliness and do not cling to his past."

1. Location controversial.

7.29 The Master said: "Is humanity so remote? If I desire humanity, there comes humanity!"[1]

1. This chapter shows that the desire to seek humanity rests with oneself.

7.30 Chen's Minister of Justice[1] asked: "Did Duke Zhao[2] know the rituals?"

Master Kong said: "Yes, he did."

Master Kong having retired, the minister cupped his hands to Wu-ma Qi[3] and approached him, saying: "I hear that the gentleman is not partial. Or is the gentleman also partial? The duke married a lady of Wu[4] who shared his family name[5] but called her Wu Meng-zi.[6] If the duke knew the rituals, who does not know the rituals?"

When Wu-ma Qi reported this, the Master said: "I am indeed fortunate! If I make a mistake, people always see it."[7]

1. Chen was a state located to the south of the present-day Kai-feng, Henan Province.
2. A former prince of Lu, reigning 541–510 B.C.E.
3. Alias of Wu-ma Shi, one of Master Kong's major disciples.
4. A large non-Chinese state of the period, with the basis of its territory in the present-day Jiangsu Province.
5. The reigning house of Lu and that of Wu, being both descended from King Wu of Zhou, inherited his family name, Ji.
6. She should be called Ji Meng-zi instead. By calling her Wu Meng-zi, the duke was trying to conceal the fact that he had married a woman with his own family name, which was in violation of the rituals.
7. To conceal the sovereign's faults was required by the rituals. But as the sage was humble and magnanimous, he readily accepted it as his mistake.

7.31 When the Master commended someone for having chanted a song well, he always made him repeat it and then chanted it in response.[1]

1. Reciprocity in all social intercourse is prescribed by the rituals.

7.32 The Master said: "In culture, perhaps I may equal others.[1] In physically conducting myself as a gentleman, however, I have not accomplished anything as yet."

1. Two variant readings of this sentence are: "In culture, I cannot surpass others" and, "In assiduity, I may equal others."

7.33 The Master said: "As for sageness and humanity, how dare I claim them? But to learn it[1] insatiably and instruct others indefatigably— that much may be said of me, that is all."

Gong-xi Hua said: "This is exactly what we disciples are unable to learn."

1. I.e., the Way of humanity.

7.34 When the Master was very sick, Zi-lu begged him to pray.

The Master said: "Is there such a practice?"

Zi-lu replied: "Yes, there is. *Eulogy*[1] says: 'Pray thou to the gods in heaven and earth.'"

The Master said: "I have prayed long enough."[2]

1. *Eulogies* is believed to have been a chapter of a book entitled *The Prayers*.
2. The Master believed that he had not sinned in any way, hence the disinclination to pray.

7.35 The Master said: "Extravagance leads to presumption; frugality leads to shabbiness. However, shabbiness is preferred to presumption."[1]

1. The criterion in the application of the rituals is the constant mean. Extravagance goes beyond the rituals and errs in being presumptuous. Frugality falls short of the rituals and errs in being shabby. Both are defects. However, shabbiness stems from simplicity (native goodness of heart), which, being the essence of the rituals, is preferred to presumption. (Cf. 3.4.)

7.36 The Master said: "The gentleman is broad-minded[1] the small man is always narrow-minded."[2]

1. Because he embraces the whole world in his love.
2. Because all that he cares about is his selfish profit. Note that the character *qi* (sad) in ancient texts is generally used to stand for *chu* (narrow or narrow-minded).

7.37 The Master looked gentle yet austere, awe-inspiring yet not fierce, respectful yet composed.[1]

1. This chapter attests to Master Kong's moderation in appearance.

Book Eight

TAI-BO

8.1 The Master said: "Tai-bo[1] may be said to be a man of supreme virtue indeed! Thrice he yielded the empire. The people could find nothing to praise him for."[2]

> 1. Prince Tai-bo, the eldest son to the First King of Zhou, the earliest ancestor of the royal house of Zhou.
> 2. Tai-bo thrice yielded the State of Zhou to his younger brother Ji-li, who begot the sage king Wen. But the way he yielded it was so secretive that the people could find nothing to praise him for. Hence the Master's approbation.

8.2 The Master said: "Respectfulness without the rituals becomes laboriousness; discretion without the rituals becomes apprehensiveness; courage without the rituals becomes rebelliousness; straightforwardness without the rituals becomes impetuosity.[1] If the gentleman[2] is devoted to his kin, the people will rise to humanity; if his old acquaintances are not abandoned, the people will not be callous."[3]

> 1. Cf. 17.7.
> 2. Referring to the emperor or the prince of a state.
> 3. Cf. 18.10.

8.3 When Master Zeng was sick, he summoned his pupils and said: "Uncover my feet; uncover my hands. *Poetry* says:

> 'Trembling with fear,
> As if standing over a deep abyss,
> As if treading on thin ice.'[1]

From now on, I know I shall be immune,[2] young men."

> 1. Lines from *The Book of Poetry, Minor Odes, Early Autumn* (See *Shi San Jing Zhu Shu*, p. 449.) The similes signify that Master Zeng had taken great

pains to protect his body from being injured as an act of filial piety, for he considered it a gift from his parents.

2. Immune from harm. As he was dying, he could no longer be harmed.

8.4   When Master Zeng was sick, Meng Jing-zi[1] went to inquire after his illness.

Master Zeng said: "When a bird is dying, its cries are mournful; when a man is dying, his words are well-meaning. The gentleman[2] values three things in the Way:[3] he modifies his appearance and manner so as to keep away from rudeness and impudence; he corrects his gaze and expression so as to stay close to truthfulness; he smoothes his speech and breathing so as to stay away from vulgar and perverse language. For such matters as ritual vessels, there are the functionaries."[4]

    1. Minister of Lu.

    2. Referring to the prince of a state or those in high positions.

    3. Here referring to the rituals.

    4. Jing-zi was liable to ignore important duties and attend to small details; hence this extra piece of advice.

8.5   Master Zeng said: "For a talented man to consult an untalented one, for a man who knows much to consult one who knows little, for a man who has to appear as if he had not, for a man who is full to appear as if he were empty;[1] for a man who has been assailed not to retaliate—formerly a friend of mine[2] applied himself to all this."

    1. "Has" and "had not" are said in regard to the Way; "full" and "empty" are said in regard to virtue.

    2. His former schoolmate Yan Hui. (Contrast 7.25.)

8.6   Master Zeng said: "A man who can be entrusted with a six-foot orphan,[1] who can be charged with the decrees of a hundred–square–li[2] state, and who, confronting a great crisis, cannot be robbed of his integrity—is he a gentleman? A gentleman indeed!"

    1. I.e., an orphaned young prince. Six ancient Chinese feet were approximately four and half modern feet. A six-foot prince would be a boy under fifteen.

    2. I.e., a large state. One *li* is approximately one third of a mile.

8.7 Master Zeng said:"A *shi*[1] cannot do without strength and stamina, for the burden is heavy and the journey long. He takes up humanity as his burden—is it not heavy? He will not stop until death—is it not long?"

  1. See 4.9, note 1.

8.8 The Master said: "Inspire yourself with *Poetry*;[1] establish yourself on *The Rituals*;[2] perfect yourself with *Music*."[3]

  1. *The Book of Poetry*. Reading about the aspirations of the ancients can inspire one's own aspirations.
  2. *The Book of Rituals*, a general code of propriety, a body of stipulations governing the rules of how to cultivate oneself, how to serve the gods and spirits, how to conduct family and social relations, and how to govern a state and the empire. (Cf. 16.13, 20.3.)
  3. *The Book of Music*, which can be used to harmonize people's feelings and perfect their character building. This book is generally believed to have been destroyed during the book-burning campaign ordered by the First Emperor of Qin in 213 B.C.E. Some scholars argue that such a book never existed.

8.9 The Master said: "The people can be made to follow it[1] but cannot be made to understand it."

  1. The sage kings' Way.

8.10 The Master said: "He who loves courage and hates poverty will rebel; he who is inhumane and is hated excessively will also rebel."

8.11 The Master said: "If a man possesses the Duke of Zhou's[1] magnificent talents but is arrogant and stingy, the rest[2] of him is not worth seeing."

  1. See 7.5, note 1.
  2. Including his talents.

8.12 The Master said: "Those who, after three years of learning, have not reached goodness, are not easy to find."[1]

  1. A variant reading of this quotation is: "Those who, after three years of learning, should never have contemplated an official's salary, are not easy to find."

8.13   The Master said: "Firmly believe in it,[1] diligently learn it, and adhere to the good Way until death.[2] A perilous state,[3] do not enter; a rebellious state,[4] do not inhabit. When the empire possesses the Way, reveal yourself;[5] when it loses the Way, conceal yourself.[6] When the state possesses the Way and you are poor and lowly, it is a shame[7] when the state loses the Way and you are rich and noble, it is also a shame."[8]

>   1. As a rule, this "it" and the one that follows both stand for the Way.
>   2. A variant reading of this sentence is: "Be sincere in truthfulness and love learning; adhere to the good Way until death."
>   3. One that portends rebellion.
>   4. One in which a minister or a prince has killed the sovereign.
>   5. Take office.
>   6. Leave office and live in seclusion.
>   7. For one should then take office to assist the good prince and thereby acquire rank and wealth.
>   8. For one should then leave office and refuse to assist the evil ruler.

8.14   The Master said: "If you are not in a certain office, do not concern yourself with its affairs."[1]

>   1. The Master advised officials to devote themselves each to his own duties. (Cf. 14.26.)

8.15   The Master said: "From Senior Music Master Zhi's[1] opening song[2] to the finale *The Melodious Chirping of the Fish Hawks*,[3]—how magnificent was the music that filled our ears!"

>   1. The chief court musician of Lu, Zhi being his name. Possibly the same court musician mentioned in 3.23 and 18.9.
>   2. According to the rituals, at court banquets and grand archery tournaments, the senior music master was supposed to open a musical program by singing the Ascension Song himself. (Cf. 3.23, note 1.)
>   3. The finale of a musical program in those days consisted of six choral pieces, all based on poems from *The Book of Poetry*. *The Melodious Chirping of the Fish Hawks* was the first of the six. For *The Melodious Chirping of the Fish Hawks*, see 3.20, note 1.

8.16   The Master said: "High-minded yet not straightforward, puerile yet not honest, sincere yet not truthful—I do not understand such people."[1]

1. The Master deplored the decline of wholehearted sincerity and truthfulness in his day.

8.17 The Master said: "In learning, if you have not reached proficiency, you are apprehensive lest you should lose it again."[1]

1. A variant reading of this quotation is: "In learning, you should feel as if unable to catch up with someone and fear that you might lose it again."

8.18 The Master said: "How lofty! Shun[1] and Yu[2] acquired the empire without participating."[3]

1. See 6.30, note 2.
2. Founding father of the Xia Dynasty, generally known as Da Yu (Yu the Great). He helped the sage king Shun to tame the Yellow River, for which Shun yielded the throne to him voluntarily.
3. I.e., without actively seeking it. Variant readings of this quotation are: "How lofty! Shun and Yu, though in possession of the empire, were totally disinterested" and "How lofty! Shun and Yu, though in possession of the empire, were not personally involved in government."

8.19 The Master said: "How great was Yao[1] as sovereign! How lofty! Heaven alone is greatest! Yao alone could imitate it! How boundless![2] The people could hardly find words to praise him! How lofty were his achievements! How brilliant his cultural institutions!"

1. See 6.30, note 1.
2. How boundless were his bounties!

8.20 Shun had five ministers, and the empire was well-ruled. King Wu[1] said: "We have ten ministers versed in government."

Master Kong said: " 'Talents are difficult to find,'[2] Is it not so? Since the period between Tang and Yu,[3] this one[4] has thriven most. But there is a woman, so, only nine.[5] Though in possession of two thirds of the empire, they still served the Yin obediently.[6] The Zhou's virtue may be said to be supreme virtue indeed!"

1. Founding father of the Zhou Dynasty (r. 1066?–1063 B.C.E.), son to King Wen, elder brother to Duke Dan and father to King Cheng, one of the ancient sage kings greatly admired by Master Kong.
2. Believed to be an ancient saying.

3. "Tang" is the name of the sage king Yao's empire, and "Yu," that of the sage king Shun's empire.

4. The Zhou Dynasty.

5. Of King Wu's ten competent ministers, one was his mother, Tai Si. Women were not supposed to take office in those days. Hence the Master's comment.

6. When King Wen, King Wu's father, was prince of the State of Zhou and overlord of the West, many states had submitted themselves to his leadership. Of the nine departments of the empire, six were under his control. Only three remained loyal to Zhou, the last emperor of the Yin Dynasty. Hence, the Master's praise.

8.21 The Master said: "Of Yu, I have nothing to censure indeed! Simple in drink and food, he was exceedingly filial to the spirits and gods.[1] Shabby in dress and skirt, he had the most beautiful sacrificial robe and crown.[2] Humble in palace and chamber, he exerted all his efforts on ditches and canals.[3] Of Yu, I have nothing to censure indeed!"

1. That is, he offered liberal sacrifices to the spirits of his ancestors as well as to the gods.

2. Fine sacrificial attire demonstrated reverence for the spirits and gods. Therefore, he scrimped on his daily garments so that he might have magnificent sacrificial robes.

3. In Yu's day, the floods had not been completely tamed. He spent huge amounts of revenues on digging ditches and canals to draw the water away so that the people might live in safety.

Book Nine

ZI HAN *(The Master Seldom)*

9.1 The Master seldom discoursed on profit, nor the decree of Heaven, nor humanity.[1]

> 1. The interpretation of this chapter is most controversial. Variant readings abound: "The Master seldom discoursed on profit; he upheld the decree of Heaven, upheld humanity;" "The Master seldom discoursed on profit except in connection with the decree of Heaven and humanity."

9.2 A man from Da-xiang Township[1] said: "How great Master Kong is! He is extensively learned, though he has not made a name in anything."

The Master, on hearing this, said to his disciples: "What shall I adhere to? Adhere to charioteering? Adhere to archery? I shall adhere to charioteering."[2]

> 1. There is no way to ascertain the location of this place now.
> 2. On hearing the man's praise, the Master responded that he would specialize in charioteering, the humblest of the Six Arts. Note the modesty and humor in these remarks.

9.3 The Master said: "Linen hats[1] are prescribed by the rituals. Nowadays people use silk ones. As they are more economical, I follow the multitude. To prostrate oneself down the hall[2] is prescribed by the rituals. Nowadays people prostrate themselves up the hall.[3] As it is presumptuous, although it goes against the multitude, I follow the down-the-hall practice."

> 1. Worn at sacrificial ceremonies in the ancestral temple, made of black linen.
> 2. At the bottom of the steps leading to the prince's audience hall.
> 3. At the audience hall above the steps.

9.4 The Master was absolutely free from four things: free from conjecture, free from arbitrariness, free from obstinacy, free from egoism.

9.5 The Master, when besieged in Kuang,[1] said: "King Wen[2] being dead, is culture not lodged here?[3] If Heaven had intended to exterminate this culture, I, a subsequent mortal, would not have been so involved in this culture. If Heaven does not intend to exterminate this culture, what can the men of Kuang do to me?"[4]

> 1. A county of Wei.
> 2. Prince of the State of Zhou (r. 1185?–1135? B.C.E.), in what is now Qi-shan County, Shaanxi Province, and overlord of the West during the later part of the Yin Dynasty; father to King Wu and Duke Dan of Zhou and one of the ancient sage kings admired most by Master Kong. The title "king" was conferred on him posthumously by his son King Wu after the founding of the Zhou Dynasty.
> 3. Referring to the Master himself.
> 4. These remarks were meant to console his disciples who were intimidated.

9.6 The prime minister asked of Zi-gong: "Is the Master a sage! How versatile he is!"[1]

Zi-gong said: "Undoubtedly it was Heaven that lavished upon him such great sageness and versatility."

The Master, on hearing this, said: "The prime minister knows me indeed! When young, I was lowly. So I became skilled in many humble occupations. Does a gentleman need many skills? No, not many."

> 1. The prime minister suspected that Master Kong was conversant only with small skills. Hence the query.

9.7 Lao[1] said: "The Master said: 'I was unemployed; therefore I became versatile.' "

> 1. Given name of Qing Zhang, one of Master Kong's major disciples.

9.8 The Master said: "Do I have knowledge? No, I have no knowledge.[1] When a country fellow asked something of me, I felt empty-like. I queried him on both ends[2] and exhausted the issue with him."[3]

> 1. Since Master Kong answered innumerable questions put to him, his contemporaries believed him to be omniscient. That is why the Master modestly said that he had no knowledge.
> 2. The beginning and the end of the matter.

3. This chapter demonstrates the Master's wholehearted sincerity in instructing others.

9.9 The Master said: "The phoenix[1] will come no more; nor will the River[2] yield the Chart.[3] I am done for!"[4]

1. The phoenix was believed to be a divine bird whose emergence portended great tranquility for the empire. It was said that a phoenix would appear only when a sage man was about to emerge.
2. Ancient name for the Yellow River, second longest river in China.
3. It was alleged that when the ancient sage king Fu-xi ascended the throne, a horse-shaped dragon emerged from the River. So he drew a chart of the Eight Diagrams in imitation of the grain of the dragon's hide and called it the River Chart.
4. The Master lamented that he would never see a sage king emerge again.

9.10 When the Master saw a man in mourning, or one wearing an official hat and suit, or a blind man—when he saw one, even a younger person, he always rose; when he passed one, he always quickened his pace.[1]

1. A sign of respect.

9.11 Yan Yuan, with a deep sigh, said: "The more I raise my eyes to it,[1] the higher it seems; the more I bore into it, the harder it becomes. I see it before me, but suddenly it is behind me.[2] However, the Master is good at guiding me on step by step, broadening me with culture and restraining me with the rituals so that even if I wanted to stop, I could not do so. Having exhausted my ability, I still seem to find something standing high above me. Though I wish to follow it, there is no way to do so."

1. The Master's Way.
2. A metaphor signifying that the Way is subtle and hard to grasp.

9.12 When the Master was critically ill, Zi-lu made some disciples serve as his house officers.[1] When he was a little better, he said: "Long indeed has Iou practiced deception! I am entitled to no house officers, but now I pretend to have them. Whom am I deceiving? Deceiving Heaven? Besides, I would rather die in your hands,[2] gentlemen, than die in the hands of house officers. And even though

I could not obtain a grand funeral,[3] would I be left in the street when I die?"

1. When a minister died, his funeral affairs were supposed to be performed by his house officers. Now that Master Kong was no longer in office, he was not entitled to any house officers. Zi-lu, being faithful to his master, made some disciples serve as his house officers so that they might perform the funeral ceremonies for him in the event of his death.

2. That is, he would rather have the disciples make funeral arrangements for him in the capacity of disciples than in the capacity of house officers.

3. An official funeral for a minister prescribed by the rituals.

9.13　Zi-gong said: "Here is a piece of beautiful jade! Shall I wrap it up and store it in a cabinet, or seek an appreciative merchant and sell it?"[1]

The Master said: "Sell it! Sell it! I am one waiting for such a merchant."

1. Zi-gong, in metaphorical terms, wanted to know whether the Master wished to conceal his accomplishments or put them to use in government.

9.14　The Master wished to live among the Nine Yis.[1]

Someone said: "They are vulgar. What can you do about them?"

The Master said: "A gentleman[2] used to live there. How could they be vulgar?"

1. There were nine Yi tribes to the East of China proper, including Korea. Some think that "the Master wished to live among the Nine Yis" and "I would board a raft and float to sea" (5.7) both express the Master's desire to go to Korea. As he was not likely to be employed in China proper, he wished to implement the Way in a foreign land.

2. Referring to the Viscount of Ji of the Yin Dynasty. (See 18.1, note 1.)

9.15　The Master said: "Only after I had returned from Wei to Lu[1] was *Music* set right and the odes and hymns restored to their proper places."[2]

1. The Master returned to Lu in the winter of the eleventh year of Duke Ai's reign (484 B.C.E.) when he was sixty-nine.

2. "Odes" and "Hymns" are two of the three sections of *The Book of Poetry*, the third being "Ballads."

9.16 The Master said: "Going out,[1] to serve the lords and ministers; coming home, to serve one's father and elder brothers; in funeral matters, not to dare to spare any efforts; not to be overwhelmed by wine—what difficulty do they present to me?"

> 1. Going to court.

9.17 The Master, standing by the river,[1] said: "That which goes by[2] is like this, without stopping day and night."[3]

> 1. Referring to either River Si or River Yi, both flowing through the State of Lu.
> 2. Referring to time.
> 3. Some scholars believe that the Master was lamenting his old age and the improbability of seeing the Way prevail. Others, however, maintain that the Master was urging his disciples to cherish their youthful time and make progress in learning incessantly.

9.18 The Master said: "I have never seen anyone who loves virtue as much as he loves beautiful women."[1]

> 1. Cf. 15.13.

9.19 The Master said: "Take, for example, building a mountain. It is left uncompleted for want of one basketful. It stopped because I stopped. Take, for example, leveling land. Though I have dumped only one basketful, it progressed because I went ahead."[1]

> 1. The Master, in metaphorical language, urged his disciples to seek progress incessantly.

9.20 The Master said: "The only one I can discourse with without ever becoming weary is perhaps Hui!"[1]

> 1. A variant reading says: "The only one I can discourse with without his ever becoming weary is perhaps Hui!"

9.21 The Master, speaking of Yan Yuan,[1] said: "Alas! I only saw him advance and never saw him stop."

> 1. After Yan Hui's death.

9.22 The Master said: "That which sprouts without flowering—there have been such cases indeed! That which flowers without fruiting—there have been such cases indeed!"[1]

> 1. In metaphorical terms, the Master again lamented the untimely death of Yan Hui.

9.23 The Master said: "Young people are awe-inspiring.[1] How do we know that in the future, they will not be so awe-inspiring as they are today?[2] However, if at forty or fifty, they remain unheard of, they will no longer be awe-inspiring."

> 1. That is because they have the potential to accumulate learning and become well cultivated in virtue.
> 2. A variant reading is: "How do we know their virtue in the future will not be so good as ours today?"

9.24 The Master said: "Upright and admonitory words—can you help accepting them? But the important thing is to correct yourself. Deferential and complimentary words—can you help liking them? But the important thing is to ruminate over them. He who likes without ruminating or accepts without correcting—I do not know what to do with him."

9.25 The Master said: "Keep wholehearted sincerity and truthfulness as your major principles. Do not befriend those beneath you. When you make a mistake, do not be afraid to correct it."[1]

> 1. Cf. 1.8.

9.26 The Master said: "The three armies[1] may be robbed of their supreme commander: but a common man cannot be robbed of his will."

> 1. See 7.10, note 2.

9.27 The Master said: "The only one who, dressed in a shabby padded hemp gown, can stand together with those dressed in fox and badger furs without feeling ashamed is perhaps Iou!"[1]

'Without envy, without greed,
How could one be anything but good?' "[2]

Zi-lu chanted these lines all his life.

The Master said: "This conforms to the Way. But how could it be considered sufficiently good?"

1. Many scholars believe that this chapter should end here and the rest is a separate chapter.

2. Lines from *The Book of Poetry, Odes of the State of Bei, The Male Pheasant.* (See *Shi San Jing Zhu Shu*, p. 302.)

9.28 The Master said: "Only when the year turns freezing cold do we realize that pines and cypresses are the last to wither."[1]

1. The metaphor signifies that only in times of crises does the integrity of the gentleman manifest itself clearly.

9.29 The Master said: "The man of wisdom is free from delusion;[1] the man of humanity is free from anxiety;[2] the man of courage is free from fear."[3]

1. For he is wise enough to discern right and wrong.

2. For he is not conscience-stricken upon self-examination and knows the decree of Heaven.

3. He does what is righteous without fear of brutal force. (Cf. 12.4, 14.28.)

9.30 The Master said: "Those who can learn with you may not be able to pursue the Way with you;[1] those who can pursue the Way with you may not be able to establish themselves with you;[2] those who can establish themselves with you may not be able to apply expediency[3] with you.

'The blossoms of the white poplar tree
Keep fluttering to and fro.
Who says I do not think of thee?
Thy house is so remote.' "[4]

The Master said: "He is not thinking of her at all. How can it be considered remote?"[5]

1. For they may be misled by heretical theories.

2. I.e., to stand firmly on the rituals with you. (Cf. 8.8, 16.13, 20.3.)

3. I.e., to depart from the rituals, the regular code of conduct, in order to achieve humanity in the event of a crisis. This is known as the doctrine of expediency. (See section on Terms, p. 26.)

4. Missing lines from *The Book of Poetry*. Metaphorically, these lines signify that the doctrine of expediency is vacillating and difficult to catch, and that the poet, though eager to acquire it feels that it is beyond his reach.

5. Also in metaphorical terms, the Master chides the poet for not being anxious enough to acquire the doctrine of expediency, for if he is, it certainly is not that difficult to learn.

Book Ten

XIANG DANG *(In His Native Place*)*

10.1   When Master Kong was in his native place, he looked simple and honest,[1] as if unable to speak. When he was in the ancestral temple and at court, he spoke eloquently, albeit discreetly.

At court when conversing with junior ministers, he looked genial and cheerful;[2] when conversing with senior ministers, he looked affable and forthright;[3] when the sovereign was present, he looked awe-stricken and moderately dignified.[4]

> 1. Two variant readings of this clause are: ". . . he looked gentle and modest, . . ." and ". . . he looked humble and prudent, . . ."
> 2. A variant reading of this clause is: ". . . he looked resolute and straightforward, . . ."
> 3. A variant reading of this clause is: ". . . he looked moderate and upright, . . ."
> 4. This section contrasts Master Kong's bearing in his native place and at court.

10.2   When the sovereign summoned him to receive guests of state, he would change his countenance and quicken his steps. He would cup his hands to those standing together with him,[1] turning his right hand to the left,[2] the front and hind hems of his robe moving up and down evenly. Then he would hasten forward like a bird unfolding its wings.[3]

When the guests had retired, he always returned to report on his mission, saying: "The guests have stopped looking back."[4]

> 1. Other courtiers appointed for the same mission.
> 2. The Master, being the leader of the reception group and standing at the head of the line on the right, had to move his right hand slightly to the left in saluting his fellow courtiers.
> 3. I.e., in a dignified manner.
> 4. This section records the Master in the execution of a mission.

*(Originally one chapter, divided into 21 sections in He Yan's ancient text.)

10.3 On entering the ducal gate, he would bend his body as if it were not tall enough to admit him. Standing, he would not do so in the middle of the gateway; walking, he would not tread the threshold. When passing the throne,[1] he would change his countenance and quicken his steps, and he seemed sparing of words.

When lifting the lower hem of his robe to ascend the audience hall, he would bend his body and abate his breath as if he had stopped breathing altogether.

On coming out and descending the first step, he would relax his features, looking cheerful. Having descended to the foot of the stairway, he would hasten forward, like a bird unfolding its wings. On regaining his position, he looked reverent.[2]

  1. The sovereign's vacant seat inside the court gate.
  2. This section records the Master's deportment at court.

10.4 Holding the jade tablet,[1] he would bend his body as if unequal to its weight. Raising it, he looked as if cupping his hands to someone; lowering it, he looked as if presenting it to someone. His countenance would change color as if trembling with fear and his feet move in quick, small steps as if tracing a marked line.[2] When presenting gifts, he looked affable. At private receptions, he looked cheerful.[3]

  1. An elongated jade ritual article held by ancient emperors and princes of states on important ceremonial occasions, pointed at the top and flat at the bottom. Its pattern and size varied with the rank of the person holding it and the occasion on which it was used. An envoy dispatched to a foreign land was also supposed to hold one at audiences with its sovereign.
  2. Signs of reverence for the host prince.
  3. This section records Master Kong's deportment as envoy at a foreign court.

10.5 The gentleman[1] would use neither reddish black nor iron gray for trimming,[2] neither scarlet nor purple to make casual wear.[3] In hot weather, he wore an unlined garment of fine or coarse hemp, always covering it with an outer garment on going out. A black smock matched a black lambskin robe;[4] a white smock, a fawnskin robe[5] and a brown smock, a fox-fur robe.[6] His fur robe for casual wear was longer than usual, with a shorter right sleeve.[7] He always had a sleeping gown,[8] one and half times the length of his body. Thick fox fur and badger fur were used to make cushions.

When mourning was removed, there was no pendant that he would not wear.[9] Except for tent skirts,[10] all fabrics had to be cut. A black lambskin robe and a black hat were not used on condolence visits. On New Year's Day, he always went to court in his court robe. When fasting, he always had clean undergarments, made of cloth.[11]

    1. Master Kong.

    2. Reddish black was the color for trimming sacrificial robes, and iron gray, for trimming three-year mourning dresses. They were not supposed to be used in trimming ordinary garments.

    3. Scarlet and purple, being mixed colors, were considered impure and unfit even for casual wear, not to mention official robes.

    4. Black robes were official robes for both the prince and his courtiers.

    5. White robes were worn by the prince and his courtiers on occasions like the prayer ceremony on the first day of each moon and receptions for foreign envoys.

    6. Brown robes were worn by the prince and his courtiers at sacrificial ceremonies.

    7. A longer casual fur robe would keep him warm, and a shorter right sleeve was convenient for work.

    8. What we call "quilt" today.

    9. In ancient times, gentlemen always wore jade pendants which symbolized virtue. However, they were supposed to be removed in mourning.

    10. Referring to skirts of official robes, made of whole bolts of fabric without cutting.

    11. This section records how Master Kong adhered to the rituals in dress matters.

10.6   When fasting, he always changed his diet,[1] and for sleeping, always moved away from his bedroom.[2]

With rice, he never ate to satiety because of its being finely pounded; with meat and fish, he never ate to satiety because of their being nicely minced. Rice that had spoiled or stank, fish that had decayed, and meat that had rotted he would not eat. Things that had discolored he would not eat. Things that smelt foul he would not eat. Things that had not been cooked right he would not eat; things that had not ripened he would not eat. Meat that had not been properly cut he would not eat. Meat that was not cooked with the right sauces he would not eat.

Even though there was plenty of meat, he would not allow himself to eat more of it than rice. Only with wine, there was no limit to quantity; but he would not drink to distraction. Purchased wine and jerky bought at the market he would not use. He never removed ginger from his food while eating but would not eat too much of it.

After sacrificing at court, he would not keep the meat overnight.[3] Other sacrificial meat he would not keep over three days. Over three days, he would not eat it.

When eating, he would not converse; lying in bed, he would not speak. Even coarse food and vegetable soup, he always offered some in sacrifice, and always in the manner of fasting.[4]

1. I.e., by abstaining from wine, ginger, onion, garlic, things that have a pungent flavour.

2. When fasting, a gentleman was not supposed to sleep with his wife or concubine.

3. A sacrificial ceremony at court usually lasted two to three days, so when the meat was distributed after the ritual to those who had taken part in it, it was already two or three days old and could not be kept any longer.

4. I.e., reverently.

This section records how the Master adhered to the rituals and sanitary regulations in food matters.

10.7 If the mat[1] was not set right, he would not sit.

When the prefecture minister was hosting the drinking ceremony,[2] he would not leave until the staff-holders[3] had left.

1. I.e., the seat. The ancients in China sat and slept on mats laid on the floor as the Japanese still do today.

2. A ceremony hosted by the prefecture magistrate, to demonstrate the significance of esteeming the worthy and feeding the aged.

3. I.e., the elders.

10.8 When the prefecture minister was observing the Exorcising Ritual,[1] he would, dressed in his court robe, stand on the eastern terrace.[2]

1. A ritual to drive away the evil spirits of pests, observed in the third moon of each year.

2. I.e., the eastern terrace of the Master's ancestral temple. That was where the head of the house was supposed to stand on such an occasion. The idea was to shield the spirits of his ancestors from being alarmed by the commotion.

10.9 When inquiring after a man[1] in a foreign land, he would prostrate himself twice on seeing the messenger off.[2]

> 1. I.e., the prince, a lord or a senior minister of that state.
> 2. Showing as much reverence for the friend as if he were present.

10.10 When Kang-zi presented him with some medicine, the Master prostrated himself in accepting it.
He said: "As I am ignorant,[1] I dare not taste it."

> 1. Ignorant of the properties of the medicine.

10.11 The stable was burnt down. When the Master retired from court, he said: "Was anyone injured?" He did not inquire about the horses.[1]

> 1. The Master valued human lives above his own property.

10.12 When the sovereign presented him with cooked food, he always set his mat right and tasted it first. When the sovereign presented him with raw meat, he always had it cooked and offered it in sacrifice. When the sovereign presented him with a living animal, he always reared it.
When he was attending upon the sovereign at a meal and the sovereign was offering sacrifice, he would first taste the food.[1]

> 1. According to the rituals, a minister dining with the prince was supposed to taste the food before the latter started to eat.

10.13 When he was ill and the sovereign came to visit him, he would lie with his head to the East,[1] covering himself with his court robe, with the girdle draped across it.

> 1. According to the rituals, the visiting prince (in this case, Duke Ai of Lu) was supposed to sit in the western part of the room and the sick subject, to lie with his head to the East, facing the prince. The western part (being the most revered part) of a room was reserved for an honored person to sit.

10.14 When the sovereign's order came to summon him, he would, without waiting for the carriage to be harnessed, start walking first.[1]

1. That is, he would walk until the carriage was harnessed and caught up with him.

10.15 When he entered the Founding Father's Temple, he inquired about everything.[1]

1. Cf. 3.15.

10.16 When a friend died and there was no shelter for his coffin, the Master said: "I shall pay for the shelter."[1]

1. The deceased friend came from a distant land, and his remains had no shelter. Hence, the Master offered to pay for the shelter of his coffin until someone came to bring it back to his homeland.

10.17 In accepting a friend's gift, be it a carriage or a horse, excepting sacrificial meat, he would not prostrate himself.

10.18 He would not sleep like a corpse, nor sit like a guest.[1]

1. A variant reading of the second half of the sentence is: "... and attend to his appearance at home."

10.19 On seeing a man in mourning, even an intimate friend, he always changed his countenance. On seeing a man wearing a ceremonial hat or a blind man, even someone close to him, he always treated him with courtesy.

To a man in funeral attire, he would bend over the horizontal bar of his carriage,[1] so would he to a man in mourning apparel.[2]

When there was sumptuous food, he always changed his countenance and rose.[3]

When there was a sudden thunderclap or a howling wind, he always changed his countenance.[4]

1. A form of salutation made by someone in a carriage.
2. A variant reading says: "So would he to a man carrying official documents."
3. A sign of thankfulness to the host.
4. A sign of awe for the wrath of heaven.

10.20 When mounting a carriage, he always stood upright, holding on to the rope.

In the carriage, he looked only at the interior.[1] He would not speak at a high pitch,[2] nor point with his finger haphazardly.[3]

1. In order not to encroach upon the privacy of those outside.
2. In order not to startle his fellow passengers.
3. In order not to puzzle the servants.
This section records how Master Kong observed the rituals in a carriage.

10.21 Startled, the bird flew away. After circling around for some time, it alighted again.

The Master said: "You female pheasant on the mountain bridge, how opportune you are! How opportune you are!"[1]

Whereby Zi-lu cupped his hands to it; the bird thrice flapped its wings and soared.[2]

1. The Master's praise for the female pheasant implied that a gentleman should act likewise: taking office and leaving office at the right time and under the right circumstances.

2. This passage is so difficult to construe that through the ages, there has been no satisfactory interpretation. Many scholars suspect errors and missing words in the text.

Book Eleven

XIAN JIN *(Those Who First Entered)*

11.1 The Master said: "Those who first entered into the rituals and music were rustics:[1] those who later entered into the rituals and music were gentlemen.[2] If I were to employ men, I would be for those who first entered into the rituals and music."[3]

> 1. Commoners who possessed neither title nor office, that is, those disciples of the Master who were children of the people and who came to the Master's school to acquire the rituals and music before taking office such as Zi-lu and Yan Hui.
> 2. Lords and ministers, that is, those disciples of the Master who were children of noble families and who inherited titles and official ranks from their fathers and elder brothers without having to acquire learning first. Later, the worthy ones of them such as Nan-gong Kuo and Meng Yi-zi who felt the need for learning entered the Master's school to acquire the rituals and music.
> 3. The Master was apparently opposed to the then prevalent hereditary system of distributing titles and official ranks and cherished a yearning to return to the ancient system of selecting worthy and talented men for office.

11.2 The Master said: "Of those who followed me in Chen and Cai,[1] none is at my door[2] now."

> 1. A small state situated to the southwest of what is now Shang-cai, Henan Province.
> 2. "Door" here means "school." The Master missed his former disciples in his old age.

11.3 Moral conduct: Yan Yuan, Min Zi-qian, Ran Bo-niu, Zhong-gong.
  Speech: Zai Wo, Zi-gong.
  State affairs: Ran You, Ji-lu.
  Literature: Zi-you, Zi-xia.[1]

> 1. A list of the disciples who excelled in the various branches of learning at Master Kong's school. "Literature" here refers to the Six Classics.

11.4 The Master said: "Hui is not one who can be of help to me.[1] In whatever I say, there is nothing he is not pleased with."

    1. That is, Hui seldom raised questions or offered advice.

11.5 The Master said: "How filial Min Zi-qian is! People have nothing censorious to say about his parents and brothers."[1]

    1. Min Zi-qian and his brother lost their mother in childhood. His father took a second wife, who bore him two more sons. The stepmother abused Zi-qian, clothing him with a reed-catkin-padded coat in winter, whereas her own sons were warmly clad in cotton-padded coats. By and by, the father discovered it and wanted to turn the stepmother out. Whereupon Zi-qian said: "If Mother stays, only one son will suffer from the cold. If Mother goes, all four sons will suffer from lack of clothing." His father was pleased and gave up the idea. Under Zi-qian's influence, the stepmother mended her ways and became a loving mother to all four children, and the brothers became friendly to one another, too. As a result, their friends and neighbors had nothing critical to say about Zi-qian's parents and his step-brothers.

    A variant reading of this sentence is: "People do not differ from what his parents and brothers have to say about him."

11.6 Nan Rong thrice recited "a white jade tablet." Master Kong gave his elder brother's daughter to him in marriage.[1]

    1. "A white jade tablet" are the key words of a stanza in *The Book of Poetry, Major State Affairs, Self-restraint* (see *Shi San Jing Zhu Shu*, p. 555):
    A stain on a white jade tablet
    May yet be rubbed away;
    A stain in our speech
    Can never be removed.
The fact that Nan Rong recited these lines repeatedly demonstrated his desire to be exceedingly discreet in speech, which, being an important virtue, pleased the Master greatly. (Cf. 5.2.)

11.7 Ji Kang-zi asked: "Which of the disciples loves learning?" Master Kong replied: "There was one Yan Hui who loved learning. Unfortunately, he died young. Now there is none."[1]

    1. Cf. 6.3

11.8   When Yan Yuan died, Yan Lu[1] requested the Master's carriage to serve as his outer coffin.[2]

The Master said: "Talented or untalented, they were each to us a son. When Li[3] died, he, too, had only an inner coffin and no outer coffin. I did not go on foot to make my carriage serve as his outer coffin. As I once followed in the wake of ministers,[4] I cannot go on foot."

1. Yan Hui's father.

2. In ancient China, a *shi* was entitled to two coffins when he died, a smaller one encased in a larger one. Here, Yan Lu was asking the Master to lend him his carriage to be used as a nominal "outer coffin" to shelter Hui's inner coffin till the day of his burial and not as a real outer coffin to be interred with his remains.

3. Master Kong's son.

4. This is Master Kong's modest way of saying that he had also served as a minister in Lu.

11.9   When Yan Yuan died, the Master said: "Alas! Heaven is killing me! Heaven is killing me!"[1]

1. Implying that by bereaving him of his only successor for the implementation of the Way, Heaven was as good as killing himself.

11.10   When Yan Yuan died, the Master lamented him excessively. His followers said: "Sir, you are grieving to excess."

The Master said: "Am I? If I do not grieve for this man excessively, for whom else should I?"

11.11   When Yan Yuan died, the disciples wanted to bury him handsomely.

The Master said: "That will not do."[1] Nonetheless, the disciples buried him handsomely.

The Master said: "Hui treated me like a father, yet I cannot treat him like a son.[2] It was not my idea. It was those gentlemen's."

1. According to the rituals, burial expenses should be in keeping with the financial status of the deceased person's family. Yan Yuan's family was poor: hence the Master's disapproval.

2. Hui's father being the rightful person to make decisions about his son's funeral arrangements, naturally the Master was not in a position to interfere.

11.12 When Ji-lu asked how to serve the spirits and gods, the Master said: "You cannot serve men yet; how can you serve the spirits?"[1]

"May I venture to ask what death is?"

The Master said: "You do not understand life yet; how can you understand death?"[2]

> 1. Spirits of one's ancestors. (Cf. 6.22.)
> 2. The Master would not discuss the unknown. (Cf. 7.20.)

11.13 Master Min, attending on one side, looked affable and upright; Zi-lu, staunch and strong; Ran You and Zi-gong, affably cheerful.[1] The Master was pleased.

"As for Iou, he is unlikely to have a natural death."[2]

> 1. The order is believed to have been arranged according to moral excellence rather than age, for Master Min was six years younger than Zi-lu.
> 2. For the times were turbulent and Zi-lu's character resolute and staunch. Master Kong's prediction unfortunately proved to be true, as Zi-lu was eventually killed in the internal strife of Wei.

11.14 The men of Lu[1] were about to rebuild the Chang Treasury. Min Zi-qian said: "Just keep it as it is—what do you think? Why rebuild it?"

The Master said: "That man seldom speaks. But when he does, he always hits the mark."[2]

> 1. Referring to the lords who controlled state affairs in Lu.
> 2. The Master commended him for trying to prevent the authorities of Lu from overtaxing the people.

11.15 The Master said: "Why does Iou play his zither at my door?"[1] Whereupon the disciples ceased to revere Zi-lu.

The Master said: "Iou has ascended to the parlor but has not entered the inner chamber yet."[2]

> 1. It was alleged that the music he made sounded militant and not harmonious; hence the Master's comment.
> 2. The various stages of progress in learning are generally represented by three metaphors: first, to enter the gate (*ru men*, i.e., to have a rudimentary knowledge of the subject); second, to ascend to the parlor (*sheng tang*, i.e., to be quite proficient in it); and third, to enter the chamber (*ru shi*, i.e., to be

highly accomplished in it). What the Master meant here is that Zi-lu had made considerable progress, but had not yet acquired the rituals and music.

11.16   Zi-gong asked: "Between Shi[1] and Shang,[2] which is the worthier?" The Master said: "Shi goes beyond whereas Shang falls short."[3] Zi-gong said: "Then Shi is the superior?" The Master said: "To go beyond is the same as to fall short."[4]

    1. Given name of the disciple Zi-zhang.
    2. Given name of the disciple Zi-xia.
    3. The unspecified object of both "goes beyond" and "falls short (of)" is "the rituals," which constitute the constant mean.
    4. For neither conforms to the constant mean. For the doctrine of the constant mean, see Terms, pp. 24–26.

11.17   Ji Shi[1] was richer than the Duke of Zhou,[2] and Qiu[3] was still amassing and collecting for him to increase his wealth. The Master said: "He is no pupil of mine. Young men, you may beat the drum and attack him."[4]

    1. Ji Kang-zi.
    2. A minister of the emperor's court, not Duke Dan of Zhou but his descendant, Master Kong's contemporary.
    3. Given name of Ran You. (See 3.6, note 4.)
    4. That is, you may attack him openly and vehemently.

11.18   Chai[1] is foolish; Shen[2] is slow-witted; Shi[3] is suave; Iou is rude.[4] The Master said: "Hui, who was close enough, often went penniless. Ci refused to accept the decree of Heaven and went into trade; his conjectures often hit the mark."[5]

    1. The disciple Gao Chai.
    2. Master Zeng.
    3. Zi-zhang.
    4. The Master's comments on the defects of four disciples.
    5. This passage contrasts Hui's and Zi-gong's attitudes toward the decree of Heaven. "Close enough" implies close enough to humanity.

11.19   When Zi-zhang asked about the way of the benevolent man,[1] the Master said: "He does not tread the beaten path[2] but will not enter the inner chamber either."[3]

The Master said: "Those who discourse sincerely are always commended. Are they real gentlemen? Or only those who assume a dignified countenance?"[4]

1. Benevolent princes. (Cf. 7.25, 13.11, 13.29.)

2. That is, he does not follow the way of government implemented by the general run of evil rulers.

3. That is, he will not acquire the rituals and music, either. (See 11.15, note 2.)

4. The relevance of joining the two paragraphs in one chapter has been controversial.

11.20　Zi-lu asked: "Should I practice something as soon as I hear it?"

The Master said: "How can you practice something as soon as you hear it when your father and eldest brother are alive?"

Ran You asked: "Should I practice something as soon as I hear it?"

The Master said: "Yes, practice it as soon as you hear it."

Gong-xi Hua said: "When Iou asked: 'Should I practice something as soon as I hear it?' Master said: 'Your father and eldest brother are alive.' But when Qiu asked: 'Should I practice something as soon as I hear it?" Master said: 'Yes, practice it as soon as you hear it.' I am puzzled. May I venture to ask why?"

The Master said: "Qiu tends to hold back;[1] therefore, I urged him on. Iou has the courage of two men; therefore, I held him back."[2]

1. See 6.12.

2. This chapter demonstrates that the Master instructed according to each disciple's shortcoming and need.

11.21　When the Master was besieged in Kuang,[1] Yan Yuan was the last to arrive.[2]

The Master said: "I thought you were dead."

Yan Yuan said: "Sir, when you are alive, how dare I die?"[3]

1. See 9.5.

2. Hui, who was following the Master in his travels, had fallen behind.

3. According to the rituals, when a man's parents are alive, he is not supposed to promise a friend to die for him. It means that Hui regarded the Master as his father.

11.22   Ji Zi-ran[1] asked: "Can Zhong Iou and Ran Qiu be called great ministers?"

The Master said: "Sir, I thought you had something else to ask. So you are asking about Iou and Qiu. Those who are called great ministers use the Way[2] to serve the sovereign. If they cannot, they should then stop. Now, Iou and Qiu may be called rank-filling ministers."[3]

Ji Zi-ran said: "Then, are they those who follow orders?"

The Master said: "In the event of patricide and regicide, they would not follow orders, either."

    1. A younger member of the noble house of Ji-sun.
    2. Referring to the rituals here.
    3. See 3.6, 11.17, & 16.1 for possible reasons for the Master's reservations about these two disciples.

11.23   When Zi-lu wanted Zi-gao to serve as magistrate of Bi,[1] the Master said: "You are ruining someone's son."[2]

Zi-lu said: "There are the people; there are the altars to the God of Earth and the God of Grains.[3] Why must the reading of books alone be considered learning?"

The Master said: "That is why I loathe glib-tongued people."

    1. Alias of the disciple Gao Chai.
    2. For Zi-gao had not completed his learning as yet.
    3. That is to say, he could learn how to govern the people and serve the gods in his office as magistrate.

11.24   When Zi-lu, Zeng Xi,[1] Ran You, and Gong-xi Hua were sitting in attendance, the Master said: "Although I may be one day your senior, do not regard me as such. Ordinarily you say: 'No one knows me!' If someone should know you, what would you do?"

Zi-lu hastily replied: "A thousand-chariot state,[2] pinched between large states, overridden by alien armies and further plagued by famine—if I were to govern it, in three years, I could make the people have courage and know the rules of propriety."

The Master smiled at him.

"Qiu, what about you?"

Ran You replied: "A state of sixty or seventy square *li*,[3] or fifty or sixty square *li*—if I were to govern it, in three years, I could make the people have plenty. As for the rituals and music, they would have to wait for the gentleman."

"Chi, what about you?"

Gong-xi Hua replied: "I am not saying I can do it, but I am willing to learn. At events in the ancestral temple such as meetings between and among princes,⁴ dressed in black robe and hat, I am willing to serve as a junior master of Ceremonies."

"Dian,⁵ what about you?"

Zeng Xi, who had been playing the zither, now slowed down. And, with a twang, he laid the zither aside and rose. Then he replied: "My aspirations are different from what the three gentlemen have stated."

The Master said: "What harm will it do? Everyone speaks his mind, that is all."

Zeng Xi said: "In late spring, when spring dresses are ready, with five or six capped men⁶ and six or seven lads, I should like to bathe in River Yi,⁷ enjoy the breeze at the Wu-yu Altar,⁸ then chant⁹ all the way home."

The Master said with a deep sigh: "I am for Dian!"¹⁰

When the three gentlemen left, Zeng Xi stayed behind. Zeng Xi said: "What do you think of the three gentlemen's statements?"

The Master said: "Well, every one spoke his mind, that is all."

Zeng Xi said: "Sir, why did you smile at Iou?"

The Master said: "One is supposed to govern a state with the rituals. His remarks were immodest. That is why I smiled at him."

"What Qiu spoke about is not a state is it?"

"How can you say that a place of sixty or seventy square *li*, or fifty or sixty square *li*, is not a state?"

"Is what Chi spoke about not a state?"

"If meetings between princes in the ancestral temple are not affairs of state, what are they? If Chi could serve only as a junior master of ceremonies, who then could serve as a senior master of ceremonies?"

1. Alias of Zeng Dian, Zeng Shen's father, one of Master Kong's earliest disciples.

2. See 1.5, note 1.

3. A medium-size state. For *li*, see 8.6, note 2.

4. Diplomatic events such as meetings between princes were held in the ancestral temple of the sovereign.

5. Given name of Zeng Xi.

6. In ancient China, young men of the *shi* class and above went through the Capping Ceremony at twenty as a token of adulthood.

7. A river flowing through the State of Lu, in what is now Shandong Province.

8. Where people prayed for rain in a drought, located on River Yi to the south of Qu-fu, the capital of Lu.

9. I.e., chant poems from *The Book of Poetry*.

10. The Master commended Zeng Xi's insight about the turbulent age and his desire to live in seclusion, further cultivate himself, and wait for the right time to emerge and take office.

12.1 When Yan Yuan asked about humanity, the Master said: " 'To restrain oneself and return to the rituals constitutes humanity.'¹ One
day one can restrain oneself and return to the rituals, all under
Heaven will turn to humanity.² The practice of humanity rests with
oneself. Does it rest with anyone else?"³

Yan Yuan said: "May I ask the details?"

The Master said: "That which does not conform to the rituals—
do not look at it; that which does not conform to the rituals—do
not listen to it; that which does not conform to the rituals—do not
say it; that which does not conform to the rituals—do not do it."

Yan Yuan said: "Slow-witted as I am, I beg to practice these
remarks."

    1. An ancient maxim.
     A variant reading of this saying is: "To be able to return to the rituals
    oneself constitutes humanity."
    2. A variant reading of this clause is: ". . . all under Heaven will commend
one as man of humanity."
    3. This is believed to be a piece of advice for the ruler.

12.2 When Zhong-gong asked about humanity, the Master said: " 'Go
abroad¹ as if you were to receive a grand guest;² employ the people
as if you were charged with a grand sacrifice.'³ 'What you do not
wish for yourself, do not impose on others.'⁴ Thus, in a state, you
will incur no resentment; in a noble house, you will incur no resentment."

Zhong-gong said: "Slow-witted as I am, I beg to practice this
saying."

    1. I.e., go to court or a noble house to perform one's duties.
    2. A guest of state.

3. This quotation which is believed to be an ancient saying means figuratively that a minister should conduct state affairs with reverence.

4. This quotation which is also believed to be an old proverb advises him to treat the people with wholehearted sincerity and like-hearted considerateness.

12.3 When Si-ma Niu[1] asked about humanity, the Master said: "The man of humanity speaks with hesitation."[2]

Si-ma Niu said: "To speak with hesitation—is that enough to be called humanity?"

The Master said: "Since to do something is difficult, can one speak about it without hesitation?"[3]

1. Alias of the Master's disciple Si-ma Geng.
2. Niu was talkative and noisy, hence the admonition.
3. Cf. 1.14, 2.13, 4.22, 4.24, 14.20, 14.27.

12.4 When Si-ma Niu asked about the gentleman, the Master said: "The gentleman is free from anxiety and fear."[1]

Si-ma Niu said: "To be free from anxiety and fear—is that enough to be called a gentleman?"

The Master said: "Since, on inward examination, he is not conscience-stricken, what anxiety and fear does he have?"

1. As his eldest brother Huan Tui, Song's minister of military affairs, was about to stage a revolt against his sovereign, Niu was living in constant anxiety and fear. Hence the Master's enlightenment. (Cf. 9.29, 14.28.)

12.5 Si-ma Niu sadly said: "Everyone else has brothers; I alone shall have none."[1]

Zi-xia said: "I heard it: 'Death and life lie with Fate; wealth and rank rest upon Heaven.'[2] If the gentleman conducts himself with reverence and does nothing amiss, if he treats others with respect and courtesy, all men within the four seas are his brothers.[3] Why should the gentleman worry about having no brothers?"

1. Niu had four brothers, the eldest being Huan Tui, Song's minister of military affairs. Tui had staged a revolt against his sovereign, and the other brothers had joined him. All four were in peril. Hence Niu's anxiety and fear.
2. This quotation has been cited as Master Kong's saying through the ages.
3. The ancients believed China to be surrounded by sea on all sides. "The four seas" has come to mean the whole empire.

12.6 When Zi-zhang asked about clear-sightedness, the Master said: "When seeping slanders and skin-pricking accusations fail to prevail on you, you may be said to be clear-sighted. When seeping slanders and skin-pricking accusations fail to prevail on you, you may even be said to be far-sighted."[1]

> 1. This is believed to be an admonition for the ruler to trust the worthy ministers in his court and to be on guard against the slanders and false accusations of those who would alienate him from them.

12.7 When Zi-gong asked about government, the Master said: "Have ample food and ample armament and the people shall trust you."

Zi-gong said: "If it is absolutely necessary to cut one item, which of the three will you cut first?"

The Master said: "Cut armament."

Zi-gong said: "If it is absolutely necessary to cut another, which of the remaining two will you cut?"

The Master said: "Cut food. Since time immemorial, all men are subject to death. If the people do not trust you, you have nothing to stand on."

12.8 Ji Zi-cheng[1] said: "What the gentleman needs is simplicity, that is all. What does he need refinement for?"[2]

Zi-gong said: "What a pity that Your Excellency should have made such a remark about the gentleman! Even a team of four horses cannot overtake the tongue.[3] Refinement is as important as simplicity; simplicity is as important as refinement. The hide of a tiger or a panther stripped of its hair is not any different from that of a dog or a sheep stripped of its hair."[4]

> 1. A minister of Wei. Nothing else is known about this man.
> 2. Simplicity signifies innate goodness of heart and refinement, accomplishment in the rituals, two indispensable qualities of a gentleman. (See Terms, pp. 29–30; cf. 6.18.)
> 3. What has been said cannot be unsaid.
> 4. Metaphorically, this means that if a gentleman (a man whose refinement and simplicity are well blended) is stripped of his refinement, he is not any different from a country fellow who possesses only simplicity but no refinement.

12.9 Duke Ai asked of You Ruo: "The year is lean, and revenues are not enough. What is to be done?"

You Ruo replied: "Why not introduce tithing?"[1]

Duke Ai said: "Even two tenths is not enough for us. How could we manage with tithing?"

You Ruo replied: "If the hundred family names[2] have enough, how can the sovereign not have enough? If the hundred family names do not have enough, how can the sovereign have enough?"

1. The levying of one tenth of the yearly produce from the land.
2. An ancient phrase standing for the common people in general.

12.10 When Zi-zhang asked how to elevate virtue and discern delusion,[1] the Master said: "Keep wholehearted sincerity and truthfulness as your major principles, and move toward righteousness—this is elevating virtue. When you love someone, you wish her to live; when you loathe her, you wish her to die. Now you wish her to live; now you wish her to die. This is delusion.

'If not for wealth,
It can only be for novelty.' "[2]

1. Cf. 12.21.
2. Lines from *The Book of Poetry, Minor State Affairs, I Walk Its Wilderness*, quoted here to censure capricious and inconstant people whose change of affection is motivated either by wealth or by the desire for novelty.

12.11 When Duke Jing of Qi[1] asked Master Kong about government, Master Kong replied: "Let a sovereign act like a sovereign, a minister like a minister, a father like a father and a son like a son."[2]

The duke said: "Well said! If indeed a sovereign acts unlike a sovereign, a minister unlike a minister, a father unlike a father and a son unlike a son, even though there was millet, how could I get to eat it?"[3]

1. Then reigning prince of Qi (r. 547–490 B.C.E.)
2. At this juncture, social order and human relations were very chaotic in Qi. Hence, the Master's reply.
3. Enlightened by the Master's statement, the duke began to realize the insecurity of his position in Qi.

12.12　The Master said: "The only one who can settle a lawsuit in a few words is perhaps Iou."[1]

Zi-lu never slept over a promise.

> 1. This chapter demonstrates Zi-lu's truthfulness in speech and resolution in action.
>
> Variant readings of this quotation are: "The only one who can settle a lawsuit on the testimony of one party is perhaps Iou" and "The only one whose testimony alone can be used to settle a lawsuit is perhaps Iou."

12.13　The Master said: "In hearing lawsuits, I may equal others. What is imperative, however, is to dispense with lawsuits."

12.14　When Zi-zhang asked about government, the Master said: "Hold it[1] without weariness; execute it with loyalty."

> 1. "It" stands for a government office in both cases.

12.15　The Master said: "He who is extensively learned in culture and restrains himself with the rituals is not likely to betray."[1]

> 1. The object of "to betray" here is understood to be "the Way." (Cf. 6.27.)

12.16　The Master said: "The gentleman helps others achieve their good ends; he does not help them achieve their evil ends. The small man does the opposite."

12.17　When Ji Kang-zi asked Master Kong about government, Master Kong replied: "Government means correctness.[1] If you take the lead in being correct, sir, who dares remain incorrect?"

> 1. In classical Chinese, the character for "government" or "to govern" is interchangeable with the character for "correctness" or "to correct." (Cf. 13.6, 13.13.)

12.18　Ji Kang-zi was troubled by theft. When he consulted Master Kong, Master Kong replied: "Sir, if you are not lustful,[1] even though you should reward them, they would not steal."

> 1. This seems to hint at Ji Kang-zi's heavy taxation and amassment of wealth. (See 11.17.)

12.19   Ji Kang-zi asked Master Kong about government, saying: "If I kill those who have lost the Way[1] to move closer to those who possess the Way[2]—what do you think of it?"

Master Kong replied: "Sir, in conducting government, why must you resort to killing? If you desire goodness, the people will be good accordingly. The gentleman's moral character is wind and the small man's moral character, grass.[3] When the grass is visited by the wind, it must surely bend."

    1. I.e., inhumane people.
    2. I.e., humane people.
    3. "The gentleman" here refers to the ruler and "the small man," the common people.

12.20   Zi-zhang asked: "What must a *shi*[1] be like to be considered distinguished?"

The Master said: "What do you mean by being distinguished?"

Zi-zhang replied: "Being always famous in a state, or always famous in a noble house."

The Master said: "That is fame, not distinction. A distinguished man is one who is upright in substance and loves righteousness, who examines people's words and observes their facial expressions, and who is anxious to remain humble to others. Such a man is always distinguished in a state and always distinguished in a noble house. A famous man, however, is one who, in appearance, upholds humanity but, in action, departs from it and who, nonetheless, arrogates it without scruples. Such a man is always famous in a state and always famous in a noble house."

    1. A virtuous scholar or minor official.

12.21   When Fan Chi accompanied the Master on an excursion to the foot of the Wu-yu Altar,[1] he said: "May I venture to ask how to elevate virtue, eliminate malice and discern delusion?"[2]

The Master said: "What a good question! Place your duties before reward[3]—is that not elevating virtue? Attack your own vices, and do not attack others' vices—is that not eliminating malice? In a fit of rage, you forget yourself and even your parents—is that not delusion?"

1. See 11.24, note 8.
2. Cf. 12.10.
3. Cf. 6.22, 15.38.

12.22　When Fan Chi asked about humanity, the Master said: "Loving men."

When asked about wisdom, the Master said: "Knowing men."

Fan Chi did not quite understand. The Master said: "Promote the upright, place them above the crooked, and you shall make the crooked upright."

Fan Chi retired and, on meeting Zi-xia, said: "A moment ago, I went to see the Master and asked him about wisdom. The Master said: 'Promote the upright, place them above the crooked, and you shall make the crooked upright.' What does it mean?"

Zi-xia said: "How rich is the statement! When Shun was in possession of the empire, he selected from the multitude and promoted Gao Yao.[1] Thus, inhumane men left him. When Tang[2] was in possession of the empire, he selected from the multitude and promoted Yi Yin.[3] Thus, inhumane men left him."

1. Minister of justice to the sage king Shun.
2. Founder of the Shang Dynasty, one of the ancient sage kings greatly admired by the Master.
3. Prime minister to the sage king Tang.

12.23　When Zi-gong asked how to associate with friends, the Master said: "Advise them with wholehearted sincerity, and guide them with goodness. If rejected, then stop. Do not bring humiliation upon yourself."

12.24　Master Zeng said: "The gentleman uses culture[1] to associate with friends; he uses friends to promote humanity."

1. Referring to the Six Classics.

13.1   When Zi-lu asked about government, the Master said: "Guide them, and make them toil.[1]"

When asked to elaborate, the Master said: "Indefatigably."

> 1. Set an example in moral conduct for the people to follow, and make them work diligently.

13.2   When Zhong-gong served as Ji Shi's magistrate,[1] he asked about government.

The Master said: "Guide the functionaries;[2] pardon minor offenses; promote worthy and talented men."

Zhong-gong said: "How do you get to know worthy and talented men to promote them?"

The Master said: "Promote those you know. As for those you do not know, will other men[3] abandon them?"

> 1. Zhong-gong once served as magistrate of Ji Shi's fief Bi County.
> 2. For "guide", see 13.1, note 1. A variant reading of this clause is: "Appoint the various functionaries first, . . ."
> 3. Other officials in leading positions.

13.3   Zi-lu said: "Sir, the prince of Wei is waiting for you to conduct his state affairs. What would you do first?"

The Master said: "It must be the rectification of characters."[1]

Zi-lu said: "Sir, how could you be so impractical! Why must you rectify characters?"

The Master said: "How boorish you are, Iou! A gentleman, confronting a character he did not know, would leave a blank space[2]. For if characters are not correct, speech will not be relevant; if speech is not relevant, affairs will not be accomplished; if affairs are not accomplished, the rituals and music will not prevail; if the rituals and music do not prevail, tortures and penalties will not be just right; if tortures and penalties are not just right, the people will not know where to put their hands and feet. Therefore, when the gentleman adopts a character, he surely can used it to say things; when he says something, it surely can be put into practice. The gentleman, in regard to his speech, is never negligent, that is all."

1. Here I follow the reading of the Han commentators. Others have read this phrase as "the rectification of names."

2. See 15.26.

13.4 When Fan Chi requested to learn farming, the Master said: "I am not as good as an old farmer."

When he requested to learn vegetable gardening, the Master said: "I am not as good as an old vegetable gardener."

When Fan Chi left, the Master said: "What a small man[1] Fan Xu is! If the sovereign loves the rituals, the people dare not be irreverent; if the sovereign loves righteousness, the people dare not be disobedient; if the sovereign loves truthfulness, the people dare not be dishonest. In that case, people from other states will flock to him with their children swaddled on their backs. What need is there for farming?"[2]

1. A commoner, or a man without high aspirations.

2. The Master pointed out that a ruler should concern himself with moral cultivation, and the rituals and music in order to implement humane government and that farming and vegetable gardening were the concerns of the common people.

13.5 The Master said: "He who can recite the three hundred poems,[1] when charged with state affairs, does not know how to handle them;[2] when dispatched as envoy to other states, cannot respond on his own[3]—though many are the poems he can recite, of what use is it?"

1. See 2.2, note 1.

2. Many poems in *The Book of Poetry* discuss state affairs, and the ideas thereof are applicable to government.

3. In ancient China, diplomatic dialogues at interstate meetings and state visits were often interspersed with quotations from *The Book of Poetry*. (See 16.13, note 3.)

13.6 The Master said: "If you yourself are correct, even without the issuing of orders, things will get done; if you yourself are incorrect, although orders are issued, they will not be obeyed."[1]

> 1. Cf. 12.17, 13.13.

13.7 The Master said: "The government of Lu and that of Wei are brothers."[1]

> 1. Both the Duke of Zhou, the founding father of Lu, and Kang-shu, the founding father of Wei, were younger sons to King Wen of Zhou. In the beginning, both states were well ruled; in Master Kong's day, however, both were ill ruled. Thus, their governments were also akin to each other.

13.8 The Master said of Prince Jing of Wei:[1] "He is good at household management. When he began to have some means, he said: 'Quite enough!' When he had a little more, he said: 'Quite sufficient!' When he had plenty, he said: 'Quite magnificent!' "[2]

> 1. A nobleman of Wei, one of the three gentlemen in that state at the time, the other two being Qu Bo-yu and Shi Qiu (see 14.25, 15.7).
> 2. The Master commended the prince for being always contented and un-covetous.

13.9 The Master journeyed to Wei, with Ran You driving.
The Master said: "How populous!"[1]
Ran You said: "Now that it is populous, what is to be done next?"
The Master said: "Enrich them."
Ran You said: "When they are rich, what is to be done next?"
The Master said: "Instruct them."

> 1. Note that populousness was an important asset to a state in ancient China, for territory was vast and population sparse, which was detrimental to agriculture. A good ruler was supposed to implement humane government so that people from other parts would flock to him. (Cf. 13.4, 13.16.)

13.10 The Master said: "If anyone employs me, in a twelvemonth, things will become tolerably well; in three years,[1] there will be notable accomplishments."

> 1. The former sage kings examined the results of their officials' work at the end of every three years.

13.11 The Master said: " 'If benevolent men[1] were to rule a state a hundred years, they would be able to tame brutes and abolish capital punishment.' How true this saying rings!"

1. Benevolent princes. (See 7.25, note 4; also cf. 11.19, 13.29.)

13.12 The Master said: "If there should emerge a sage man, it would surely take a generation[1] for humanity to prevail."

1. Thirty years.

13.13 The Master said: "If you can set yourself correct, what difficulty do you have in conducting state affairs? If you cannot set yourself correct, how can you correct others?"[1]

1. Cf. 12.17, 13.6.

13.14 When Master Ran returned from court,[1] the Master said: "Why so late?"

Master Ran replied: "There was some state affair."

The Master said: "It must have been some house affair.[2] If it had been a state affair, even though I am no longer employed, I would have been informed about it."

1. Ji Kang-zi's private court. Ran You was serving as Ji-sun's chief house officer at the time.
2. Some affair of the noble house of Ji-sun.

13.15 Duke Ding[1] asked: "One remark that can prosper a state—is there such a thing?"

Master Kong replied: "One remark cannot do something like that. However, there is one close to it. One man's saying goes: 'To be a sovereign is difficult; to be an official is not easy either.'[2] If one knows the difficulty of being a sovereign, is it not almost true that one remark can prosper a state?"

Duke Ding said: "One remark that can lose a state—is there such a thing?"

Master Kong replied: "One remark cannot do something like that. However, there is one close to it. One man's saying goes: 'I find no joy in being a sovereign except that, whatever I say, no one disobeys me.'[3] If what he says is good and no one disobeys him, is it not good? If it is not good and no one disobeys him, is it not almost true that one remark can lose a state?"

1. See 3.19, note 1.
2. This saying is attributed to Duke Wen of Jin (r. 636–628 B.C.E.) of the Spring and Autumn period.
3. This saying is attributed to Duke Ping of Jin (r. 557–532 B.C.E.) of the same period.

13.16 When the Duke of She[1] asked about government, the Master said: "Make those nearby pleased and those far off flock to you."

1. See 7.18, note 1.

13.17 When Zi-xia served as magistrate of Ju-fu,[1] he asked about government.

The Master said: "Do not crave for speed; do not covet petty gains. If you crave for speed, you will not reach your destination; if you covet petty gains, great undertakings will not be accomplished."

1. A county of Lu, located to the southeast of the present-day Gao-mi, Shandong Province.

13.18 The Duke of She said to Master Kong: "In my native place, there is a man nicknamed Straight Body. When his father stole a sheep, he bore witness against him."

Master Kong said: "In my native place, straight people are different from this man: Father conceals for son and son conceals for father. Straightness lies therein."

13.19 When Fan Chi asked about humanity, the Master said: "Conduct yourself with respect; perform your duties with reverence; treat others with wholehearted sincerity. Even if you should journey to the Yis and Dis,[1] you cannot abandon these."

1. See 3.5, note 1.

13.20 Zi-gong asked: "What must a man be like to be called a *shi*?"[1]

The Master said: "In conducting himself, he has a sense of

shame;[2] when dispatched to the various states as envoy, he does not fail the sovereign's mission—such a man may be called a *shi*."

Zi-gong said: "May I venture to ask the next category?"

The Master said: "One who is commended as a filial son in his own clan and an obedient younger brother in his native place."

Zi-gong said: "May I venture to ask the third category?"

The Master said: "One whose word is always truthful and whose deed is always resolute. Inflexible small man that he is, he may yet be considered one of the third category."

Zi-gong said: "What about those engaged in government today?"

The Master said: "Ugh! Those men of small capacity—they are not worth reckoning."

1. See 4.9, note 1.

2. That is to say, they would not condescend to do evil things.

13.21   The Master said: "Unable to find men of the middle path[1] to associate with, I must content myself with the high-minded and the principled. The high-minded forge ahead, and the principled refrain from doing certain things."[2]

1. Men whose conduct conforms to the constant mean.

2. This is believed to have been said in connection with the Master's criterion for selecting students.

13.22   The Master said: "The Southern Man[1] had a saying that goes: 'If a man is inconstant, he should not have his fortune divined.'[2] Well said!

He who is inconstant in moral character

Will always incur humiliation."[3]

The Master said: "He should never try divination, that is all."[4]

1. *Li Ji, Zi Yi* (*Records of the Rituals, Black Dress*), says this is the title for the head official of divination in the Yin Dynasty. (See *Shi San Jing Zhu Shu*, p. 1651.)

2. It means that his fortune is bound to be inauspicious. Ibid.

3. The Master again quoted from *Yi Jing, Xi Ci, Heng Gua* (*The Book of Changes, Appended Interpretations, The Diagram of Constancy*, in *Shi San Jing Zhu Shu*, p. 47) to support his own argument. I have consulted the text of *Li Ji, Zi Yi* for a more relevant rendition of this chapter.

4. In this chapter, the Master tried to prove that a man inconstant in virtue would incur bad luck.

13.23 The Master said: "The gentleman is harmonious but not comformable; the small man is conformable but not harmonious."[1]

1. The gentleman embraces all in his humanity; hence, he is harmonious at heart; but when he differs from others on matters of moral principle, he does not give up his opinion to oblige others. The small man is contentious in seeking profit, so he is not harmonious; but as he does not care about any moral principles, he readily gives up his own ideas to oblige others.

Note that the gentleman and the small man are differentiated by virtue in this chapter.

13.24 Zi-gong asked: "The people of the prefecture all love him—What do you think about such a man?"

The Master said: "Not good enough."

"The people of the prefecture all loathe him—what do you think about such a man?"

The Master said: "Not good enough, either. It would be best if the prefecture's good people loved him and its evil people loathed him."[1]

1. Cf. 15.28.

13.25 The Master said: "The gentleman is easy to serve but hard to please. If you do not please him according to the Way, he is not pleased. When he employs a person, he measures his capacity. The small man is hard to serve but easy to please. Even though you do not please him according to the Way, he is pleased. When he employs a person, he demands perfection."[1]

1. Again, the gentleman and the small man are differentiated by virtue here.

13.26 The Master said: "The gentleman is self-possessed and not swaggering; the small man is swaggering and not self-possessed."[1]

1. The demarcation line between the two kinds of men here is also virtue.

13.27 The Master said: "Staunchness, stamina, simplicity, and reticence are close to humanity."

13.28 Zi-lu asked: "What must a man be like to be called a *shi*?"

The Master said: "One who is sincerely critical and genial may be called a *shi*—sincerely critical to his friends, genial to his brothers."

13.29 The Master said: "After a benevolent man[1] instructs the people for seven years, they may be employed to take arms."

1. A benevolent prince. (Cf. 7.25, 11.19, 13.11.)

13.30 The Master said: "To employ uninstructed[1] people in battle is to abandon them."

1. The instruction implied here includes instruction in the rituals and righteousness as well as military training.

Book Fourteen

XIAN WEN *(Xian Asked)*

14.1   When Xian[1] asked about shame, the Master said: "When the state possesses the Way, you draw an official's salary; when the state loses the Way, you draw an official's salary—it is a shame."[2]

"To be able to prevent the desire to outdo others, bragging, resentment, and greed from prevailing—can this be considered humanity?"

The Master said: "It may be considered difficult. As for humanity, I do not know."

> 1. Given name of the disciple Yuan Si.
> 2. Cf. 8.13.

14.2   The Master said: "If a *shi* cherishes home life, he is unfit to be a *shi*."[1]

> 1. A high-minded *shi* should seek office and implement the Way wherever he is needed and not indulge in the comfort of home life.

14.3   The Master said: "When the state possesses the Way, speak uprightly and act uprightly; when the state loses the Way, act uprightly, but speak modestly."[1]

> 1. His conduct does not change, but he speaks modestly to stay out of harm's way.

14.4   The Master said: "A man who possesses virtue must also possess worthy sayings, but a man who possesses worthy sayings does not necessarily possess virtue. A man of humanity must also possess courage, but a man of courage does not necessarily possess humanity."

14.5   Nan-gong Kuo[1] asked of Master Kong, saying: "Neither Yi, who was skilled in archery, nor Ao, who excelled in maneuvering battleships, met a natural death.² Right? Yu and Ji, however, who grew crops themselves, gained possession of the empire."³

The Master did not reply.⁴

When Nan-gong Kuo left, the Master said: "What a gentleman that man is! How that man upholds virtue!"

1. The disciple Nan Rong.

2. Yi, the prince of a small state during the Xia Dynasty who usurped the throne from the emperor of Xia; Ao, the son of another usurper. Both men were unrighteous and upheld force.

3. For Yu, see 8.18, note 2. Ji, also known as Hou Ji, is believed to be a remote ancestor of the Zhou Dynasty who served as minister of agriculture to the sage king Yao. Both Yu and Ji were revered as men of great virtue.

4. As Nan-gong's remarks implicitly compared Master Kong to Yu and Ji, the Master modestly refrained from replying.

14.6 The Master said: "A gentleman who is not humane—there are such cases, indeed. But there has never been one case in which a small man is humane."¹

1. The two categories are still differentiated by virtue.

14.7 The Master said: "Can you love them without making them toil? Can you be loyal to him without admonishing him?"¹

1. This was said in regard to an official's duty to the people and to the sovereign.

14.8 The Master said: "In preparing a diplomatic dialogue, Bi Chen was the one to ride to the country and draft it;¹ shi shu,² the one to study and comment on it; Foreign Minister Zi-yu, the one to revise and decorate it; and East-neighborhood Zi-chan,³ the one to polish and color it."

1. Bi Chen, minister of Zheng, was in the habit of going to the country, away from the distractions of the capital, to draft diplomatic documents. (See *Zuo's Commentary on the Spring and Autumn Annals, Duke Xiang,* 31st year, in *Shi San Jing Zhu Shu,* p. 2015.)

2. Minister of Zheng, whose name was You Ji.

3. Prime minister of Zheng. (See 5.16, note 1.) Note that East-neighborhood, the location of his residence, had become part of his name.

This chapter demonstrates Zi-chan's ability to choose the right people for the right jobs.

14.9 When someone asked about Zi-chan, the Master said: "A beneficent man."

When asked about Zi-xi,[1] he said: "Oh, that man! Oh, that man!"[2]

When asked about Guan Zhong,[3] he said: "A humane man. He deprived Bo Shi[4] of the three hundred households of Pian County[5] so that Bo Shi could eat only coarse food. Until the end of his life, however, he never uttered one resentful word."[6]

1. Some scholars believe this man to be Prince Shen of Chu, alias Zi-xi, prime minister to King Zhao of Chu. He had prevented the king from granting Master Kong a gift of land during the Master's visit to that state.

2. The Master refrained from commenting on someone who had done him an ill turn.

3. See 3.22, note 1. Also cf. 14.16, 14.17.

4. Bo Yan, minister of Qi, who had committed a major offense, for which he forfeited the taxes of the three hundred households of his fief Pian County.

5. In what is now Lin-qu, Shandong Province.

6. For the penalty was just and reasonable.

14.10 The Master said: "To be poor and not resentful is difficult; to be rich and not swaggering is easy."

14.11 The Master said: "Meng Gong-chuo,[1] as chief house officer of Zhao or Wei,[2] would be more than proficient, but could not serve as a minister of Teng or Xue."[3]

1. Minister of Lu, known to be an uncovetous man. (Cf. 14.12.)

2. Two of the three prominent noble houses in control of state power in Jin, the other being the noble house of Han.

3. Two small states in the Spring and Autumn period.

14.12 When Zi-lu asked about the perfect man, the Master said: "A man with Zang Wu-zhong's[1] wisdom, Gong-chuo's[2] uncovetousness, Bian Zhuang-zi's[3] courage, Ran Qiu's versatility,[4] and further refined with the rituals and music, may be considered a perfect man indeed."

The Master said: "A perfect man of today—why must he be like that? One who, on seeing profit, thinks of righteousness; on seeing danger, is ready to give his life; and, even with an old agreement, does not forget his former promise may yet be considered a perfect man."

1. Son to Zang Wen-zhong (5.18, note 1); minister of Lu.
2. See 14.11, note 1.
3. Minister of Bian County in Lu, known to have killed a tiger single-handed.
4. See 6.8.

14.13 The Master asked Gong-ming Jia[1] about Gong-shu Wen-zi,[2] saying: "Is it true that His Excellency neither speaks, nor laughs, nor takes?"

Gong-ming Jia replied: "This is the informant's error. His Excellency speaks only at the right time so that people are not weary of his speech, laughs only when he is happy so that people are not weary of his laughter, and takes only when it is righteous so that people are not weary of his taking."

The Master said: "Is that so? Is it really so?"

1. Native of Wei and house officer to Gong-shu Wen-zi. Nothing much is known about this man.
2. Gong-sun Ba, grandson to Duke Xian of Wei (r. 576–559 B.C.E.), "Wen" being his posthumous title; a worthy minister of Wei.

14.14 The Master said: "Zang Wu-zhong[1] used Fang[2] to demand that an heir be appointed for him in Lu.[3] Although people say he did not coerce the sovereign, I do not believe it."

1. See 14.12, note 1.
2. Zang Wu-zhong's fief, bordering on the State of Qi.
3. As minister of justice in Lu, Zang was maligned by Meng-sun to the prime minister, Ji-sun, who gave orders to attack him. He escaped to his fief Fang County, which he seized and held hostage until his nephew Wei was appointed his heir in Lu.

14.15 The Master said: "Duke Wen of Jin was crafty and not upright;[1] Duke Huan of Qi was upright and not crafty."[2]

1. The second of the five overlords of the Spring and Autumn period (r. 636–628 B.C.E.). To parade his authority, he once summoned the emperor of

Zhou to He-yang, a city of Jin, for a meeting and made him participate in a hunting game there.

2. The very first of the five overlords of the same period (r. 685–643 B.C.E.) He once sent a punitive expedition against the non-Chinese state Chu because it had stopped paying tribute to the emperor of Zhou. To uphold the prestige of the royal house of Zhou was considered the first and foremost obligation of the overlord.

14.16   Zi-lu said: "When Duke Huan killed Prince Jiu,[1] Shao Hu[2] died for him, but Guan Zhong[3] did not die." He added: "He was not humane, was he?"

The Master said: "Duke Huan nine times assembled the various princes without using war chariots. It was all Guan Zhong's capability. Who can compare with him in humanity? Who can compare with him in humanity!"

1. Elder brother to Duke Huan of Qi who had him assassinated in the contention for the throne.

2. One of Prince Jiu's two tutors, the other being Guan Zhong.

3. See 3.22, note 1; also cf. 14.9, 14.17.

14.17   Zi-gong said: "Guan Zhong was not a man of humanity, was he? When Duke Huan killed Prince Jiu, he not only was unable to die but became the duke's prime minister, instead."

The Master said: "Guan Zhong helped Duke Huan become overlord of the various princes and set everything right in the empire. The people to this day benefit from his favors. But for Guan Zhong, we would be wearing our hair loose with our garments fastened on the left.[1] How could we expect him to be obstinately truthful like a common man or a common woman and hang himself in a gully without anyone knowing about it?"

1. Customs of barbarian tribes.

14.18   Gong-shu Wen-zi's[1] house minister[2] Xun was, together with Wen-zi, promoted to the ducal court. The Master, on hearing this, said: "He deserves to be called 'Wen'[3] indeed!"

1. See 14.13, note 2.

2. Officials in noble houses were also divided into two categories: ministers and *shi* (minor officials).

3. *Wen*, which means "refined," was part of Gong-shu's posthumous title.

14.19   The Master said: "Long indeed has Duke Ling of Wei[1] lost the Way!"

Kang-zi said: "In that case, why did he not lose his state?"

Master Kong said: "He had Zhong-shu Yu[2] to manage affairs of protocol, Zhu Tuo[3] to manage the ancestral temple, and Wang-sun Jia[4] to manage the armed forces. In that case, how could he lose his state?"

    1. Then reigning prince of Wei. He was Master Kong's host for many years during the Master's travels abroad but was unable to employ him as he was completely overwhelmed by military force and women, his two ruling passions.

    2. Referring to Kong Wen-zi. (See 5.15, note 1.)

    3. See 6.16, note 1.

    4. See 3.13, note 1. All three were competent men, well qualified for their respective posts.

14.20   The Master said: "If one speaks unabashedly, he will find it difficult to practice."[1]

    1. Cf. 1.14, 2.13, 4.22, 4.24, 12.3, 14.27.

14.21   Chen Cheng-zi[1] assassinated Duke Jian.[2] Master Kong, after bathing himself,[3] went to court and reported to Duke Ai, saying: "Chen Heng has assassinated his sovereign. Pray send a punitive expedition against him."

The duke said: "Report to those gentlemen."[4]

Master Kong said: "As I once followed in the wake of the ministers, I dared not refrain from reporting. And the sovereign said: 'Report to those gentlemen.'"

He went and reported to those gentlemen, who disapproved.

Master Kong said: "As I once followed in the wake of the ministers, I dared not refrain from reporting."

    1. Posthumous title of Chen Heng, minister of Qi, also known as Tian Chang.

    2. Then reigning prince of Qi.

    3. According to the rituals, before an audience with the sovereign, a minister was supposed to fast and bathe himself.

    4. That is, the three leading consuls in the court of Lu, namely, the heads of the noble houses of Ji-sun, Meng-sun, and Shu-sun.

14.22 When Zi-lu asked how to serve the sovereign, the Master said: "Do not deceive him, but you may confront him."

14.23 The Master said: "The gentleman perceives higher things: the small man perceives lower things."[1]

> 1. Cf. 4.16
> A variant reading of this quotation is: "The gentleman reaches for higher things; the small man reaches for lower things."

14.24 The Master said: "The scholars of antiquity learnt for themselves; the scholars of today learn for others."[1]

> 1. "To learn for oneself" means to acquire the Way in order to practice it; "to learn for others" means merely to brag about it to other people.

14.25 When Qu Bo-yu[1] sent a messenger to Master Kong, Master Kong sat with him and asked: "What has His Excellency been doing?"

The messenger replied: "His Excellency wishes to make fewer mistakes but has not succeeded as yet."

When the messenger left, the Master said: "What a messenger! What a messenger!"[2]

> 1. A worthy minister of Wei. He acted as Master Kong's host during one of the latter's visits to Wei.
> 2. The Master praised the messenger for his truthful and modest report about his master.

14.26 The Master said: "If you are not in a certain office, do not concern yourself with its affairs."[1]

Master Zeng said: " 'The gentleman does not think beyond his office.' "[2]

> 1. Cf. 8.14.
> 2. See *The Book of Changes*, Vol. V, *Diagram of Stoppage,* (see *Shi San Jing Zhu Shu*, pp. 62–63).

14.27 The Master said: "The gentleman deems it shameful if his speech exceeds his action."[1]

> 1. Cf. 1.14, 2.13, 4.22, 4.24, 12.3, 14.20.

14.28 The Master said: "There are three things in the gentleman's Way that I am incapable of: the man of humanity is free from anxiety; the man of wisdom is free from delusion; the man of courage is free from fear."[1]

Zi-gong said: "This is the Master's self-portrayal."

    1. Cf. 9.29, 12.4.

14.29 When Zi-gong was disparaging someone, the Master said: "Ci, are you good enough now? As for me, I do not have the leisure."

14.30 The Master said: "Do not worry about men not knowing you; rather, worry about your incapability."[1]

    1. Cf. 1.16, 4.14, 15.19.

14.31 The Master said: "He who neither presupposes deception nor suspects untruthfulness, yet discerns it all beforehand, is worthy indeed!"

14.32 Wei-sheng Mu[1] said to Master Kong: "Qiu, why are you so restless? Are you not parading your eloquence?"[2]

Master Kong said: "Not that I dare parade my eloquence, but that I am troubled by the benightedness."[3]

    1. Native of Lu, possibly a hermit.
    2. Referring to Master Kong's travels through the various states in search of a wise prince to employ him.
    3. That is, the world's ignorance about the Way.

14.33 The Master said: "A thousand-*li* horse is praised not for its strength, but for its virtue."[1]

    1. A metaphor signifying that a good prince was praised for his virtue and not for his military strength. (Cf. 16.12.)

14.34 Someone said: " 'Requite enmity with favor.'[1] What do you think of that?"

The Master said: "Then, how do you requite favor? Requite enmity with impartiality; requite favor with favor."

1. This is upheld by Lao Tzu in the *Tao Te Ching*, Ch. 63. He believes it to be the only way to eliminate enmity among men.

14.35 The Master said: "Nobody will ever understand me!"

Zi-gong said: "Why will nobody ever understand you, sir?"

The Master said: "I neither resent Heaven nor blame men.[1] I learnt lower things and perceive higher things.[2] The only one who understands me is perhaps Heaven!"

1. Although he was not employed, he did not resent Heaven; although the princes of the day did not appreciate his accomplishments, he did not blame them.

2. "Lower things" refers to human affairs, and "higher things", to such things as the decree of Heaven.

14.36 Gong-bo Liao[1] slandered Zi-lu before Ji-sun.[2] Zi-fu Jing-bo[3] reported it, saying: "His Excellency[4]'s mind is undoubtedly deluded. As for Gong-bo Liao, I still have power enough to have his corpse exposed at the market place or at court."[5]

The Master said: "That the Way shall prevail rests with the decree of Heaven; that the Way shall fail also rests with the decree of Heaven. What can Gong-bo Liao do to the decree of Heaven?"

1. See Master Kong's Major Disciples, p. 206.

2. Ji Kang-zi, see 2.20, note 1.

3. Zi-fu He, see Master Kong's Major Disciples, p. 207.

4. Ji Kang-zi.

5. According to the laws of the Zhou Dynasty, after an execution, the corpse of the executed person was to be exposed at the market place if he was a *shi* or at court if he was a minister.

14.37 The Master said: "Worthy men flee the world;[1] the next category flee a place;[2] the third category flee a facial expression;[3] the fourth category flee a remark.[4]"

The Master said:[5] "Those who did so numbered seven."[6]

1. They shunned office altogether in a chaotic epoch.

2. They left an ill-ruled state for a well-ruled one.

3. They left office when the prince's courtesy began to slacken.

4. They left office when the prince said something discourteous.

5. The repetition of "The Master said" suggests that the final remark may have been made on a different occasion.

6. Some believe them to be the Taoist hermits mentioned in *Lun Yu*, namely: Chang-ju and Jie-ni (18.6), the old man (18.7), the morning gate-keeper (14.38), the basket-bearer (14.39), the frontier warden of Yi County (3.24), and Chu's Madman Jie-yu (18.5). Others believe them to be Bo-yi, Shu-qi, Yu-zhong, Yi-yi, Zhu-zhang, Liu Xie-hui, and Shao-lian. (See 18.8.)

14.38 Zi-lu lodged at Stone Gate.¹ The morning gate-keeper said: "Where from?"

Zi-lu said: "From Kong Shi's place."

The gate-keeper said: "Is it the man who knows it cannot be done yet keeps trying?"²

1. The city gate of Qu-fu, the capital of Lu.
2. The man was mocking Master Kong for bustling about restlessly in search of a wise prince.

14.39 The Master was striking the chime stone in Wei. A bearer of baskets, passing by Kong Shi's door, said: "Heavy-laden is the chime stone player!" A moment later, he said: "How despicable! Keng! Keng!¹ Since nobody knows you, stop trying, that is all.

When deep, wade with garments unlifted;
When shallow, wade with garments uplifted."²

The Master said: "How resolute! To him, nothing seems difficult."

1. Mimicking the sound of the chime.
2. From *The Book of Poetry, Ballads of the State of Bei, The Gourd Has Bitter Leaves*. (See *Shi San Jing Zhu Shu*, p. 302.) The implication is that one should be flexible and adapt one's actions to the circumstances. The basket-bearer was satirizing the Master's tenacity in attempting to reform the world in such a chaotic epoch.

14.40 Zi-zhang said: "*History* says: 'Gao-zong,¹ in his mourning hut,² for three years did not speak.'³ What does it mean?"

The Master said: "Why must it be Gao-zong? Men of antiquity⁴ all did the same. After a king's demise, the hundred officials⁵ assumed total responsibility over their own departments, submitting themselves to the jurisdiction of the prime minister for three years."

1. King Wu-ding (r. 1324?–1264? B.C.E.) of the Yin Dynasty.
2. According to the rituals, a bereaved son was supposed to live in a straw

hut for three years, sleeping on a stalk mat and using a piece of earth for a pillow.

3. See *The Book of History, Sans Ease*, in *Shi San Jing Zhu Shu*, p. 221.

4. "Men of antiquity" refers to all ancient kings.

5. "The hundred officials" refers to the officialdom as a whole.

14.41   The Master said: "If the sovereign loves the rituals, the people will be easy to employ."

14.42   When Zi-lu asked about the gentleman,[1], the Master said: "He cultivates himself in reverence."[2]

Zi-lu said: "Is that all?"

The Master said: "He cultivates himself in bringing peace to men."[3]

Zi-lu said: "Is that all?"

The Master said: "He cultivates himself in bringing peace to the hundred family names.[4] To cultivate oneself in bringing peace to the hundred family names—even Yao and Shun found it difficult."

1. Here referring to the sovereign.

2. The first step of the gentleman's cultivation is to cultivate himself in acquiring the rituals and revering himself.

3. The second step is to cultivate himself in bringing peace to the nobility. "Men" here refers to his clan, hence the nobility.

4. The third step is to cultivate himself in bringing peace and good order to all the people in the empire.

14.43   Yuan Rang[1] sat with his legs outstretched, waiting. The Master said: "When young, you were immodest and disobedient; when grown up, you had nothing to recommend you; when old, you refuse to die. You are indeed a pest!" And, with his staff, he tapped him on the shank.

1. Yuan Rang was an old acquaintance of the Master, native of Lu. It was alleged that when his mother died, he climbed upon her coffin and sang. Throughout his life he defied the rituals and conventions.

14.44   A lad from Que Township[1] served as go-between.[2] Someone asked the Master, saying: "Is he one seeking progress?"

The Master said: "I saw him ensconced in a seat;[3] I saw him walking side by side with his elders.[4] He is not one seeking progress but one eager to become an adult."

1. A village at the Que Gate of Qu-fu, where Master Kong had his residence.

2. According to the rituals, when one *shi* wished to meet another for the first time, the request for the meeting, the exchange of gifts, and the dialogue between the guest and the host were all conducted through a go-between.

3. Lads were supposed to sit in the corner of a room without occupying seats. Seats were reserved for adults.

4. According to the rituals, lads were supposed to walk behind their elders.

Book Fifteen

WEI LING GONG *(Duke Ling of Wei)*

15.1　When Duke Ling of Wei[1] asked Master Kong about battle array, Master Kong replied: "Of ritual affairs, I have heard some; of military affairs, I have learnt nothing." The following day, he departed.

> 1. See 14.19. note 1.

15.2　In Chen,[1] they ran out of food. The followers became so weak that none could rise. Zi-lu, with conspicuous resentment, said:[2] "So, the gentleman is also susceptible to adversity?"

The Master said: "The gentleman rests at ease in adversity; the small man, once reduced to adversity, becomes reckless."

> 1. See 5.22, note 1.
> 2. A variant reading of this clause is: "Zi-lu, resentful, went to see the Master, saying: . . ."

15.3　The Master said: "Ci, do you regard me as someone who learns much and commits it all to memory?"

Zi-gong replied: "Yes. Are you not?"

The Master said: "No, I use one string to thread it all together."[1]

> 1. Wholehearted sincerity and like-hearted considerateness which is sometimes equated with humanity.

15.4　The Master said: "Iou, those who know virtue are rare indeed!"[1]

> 1. This is believed to be a comment on the event that occurred in 15.2.

15.5　The Master said: "The only one who achieved good government through nonaction was perhaps Shun![1] For what did he do? He conducted himself respectfully facing due south, that is all."

1. See 6.30, note 2. Master Kong's idea of nonaction might have been impacted by Lao Zi's, but they are basically different and not to be confused one with the other.

15.6 When Zi-zhang asked how to get on in the world, the Master said: "If your speech is wholeheartedly sincere and truthful and your deeds honest and reverent, even in barbarian states, you will get on. If your speech is neither wholeheartedly sincere nor truthful, and your deeds neither honest nor reverent, even in your native place, can you get on? Standing, you seem to see these tenets greeting you in front; in a carriage, you see them leaning against the yoke.[1] Only then will you get on."

Zi-zhang wrote it down on his girdle.

1. That is, you should always bear these tenets in mind.

15.7 The Master said: "How straight Shi Yu[1] was! When the state possessed the Way, he was like an arrow; when the state lost the Way, he was like an arrow. What a gentleman Qu Bo-yu[2] is! When the state possessed the Way, he took office; when the state lost the Way, he was able to roll it up and pocket it."[3]

1. A worthy minister of Wei, known for his straightness.
2. See 14.25, note 1.
3. "It" stands for his moral accomplishment in both cases.

15.8 The Master said: "If a man is worth talking[1] to and you do not talk to him, you lose a man; if a man is not worth talking to and you talk to him, you lose your words. The man of wisdom neither loses a man nor loses his words."

15.9 The Master said: "Lofty-minded *shi* and humane men do not seek to preserve their lives at the expense of humanity; rather, they give their lives to attain humanity."[1]

1. E.g., in the case of saving a child out of a conflagration.

15.10 When Zi-gong asked how to cultivate humanity, the Master said: "If an artisan wishes to perfect his craft, he must first sharpen his tools.[1] Living in this state, serve the worthy of its ministers and befriend the humane of its *shi*."

1. The interpretation of the metaphor lies in the statement that follows. (Cf. 12.24.)

15.11 When Yan Yuan asked how to govern a state, the Master said: "Follow the Xia calendar,[1] ride in the Yin coach, and wear the Zhou crown.[2] As for music, imitate *The Succession* and *Military Exploits*.[3] Ban the songs of Zheng and keep away from glib-tongued men. For the songs of Zheng are obscene and glib-tongued men dangerous."

> 1. The calendar of the Xia Dynasty, also known as the Lunar Calendar or the farmer's calendar, serves the farmer far better than any other calendar ever adopted in China. To this day, it is still widely followed in rural areas.
> 2. The Yin emperor's coach was much simpler and sturdier than the Zhou emperor's; the Zhou crown, on the other hand, was more elaborately decorated. In mundane matters the Master preferred simplicity to ostentation, but he upheld splendor in ritual attire.
> 3. See 3.25, note 1.

15.12 The Master said: "If a man does not have long-range considerations, he will surely incur imminent afflictions."

15.13 The Master said: "It is all over! I have never seen anyone who loves virtue as much as he loves beautiful women."[1]

> 1. Cf. 9.18.

15.14 The Master said: "Zang Wen-zhong was indeed a usurper of his office! Knowing Liu-xia Hui's worth, he would not give him a position."[1]

> 1. As minister of justice and Liu-xia's superior, Zang was in a good position to know the latter's worth and promote him to a higher position, but he refrained from doing so.

15.15 The Master said: "Be more demanding with yourself and less so with others and you shall keep resentment away."[1]

> 1. Cf. 15.21.

15.16 The Master said: "Those who never say 'What to do? What to do?'[1]—I do not know what to do with them indeed!"

1. This is said about people who never think about anything carefully before doing it.

15.17 The Master said: "Those who herd together all day without talking about anything that touches upon righteousness and love to display their petty cleverness are difficult[1] indeed!"

1. I.e., difficult to instruct in the Way. (Cf. 17.21.)

15.18 The Master said: "A gentleman considers righteousness his major principle: he practices it in accordance with the rituals, utters it in modest terms, and fulfils it with truthfulness. A gentleman indeed!"

15.19 The Master said: "The gentleman worries about his incapabilty; he does not worry about men not knowing him."[1]

1. Cf. 1.16, 4.14, 14.30.

15.20 The Master said: "What the gentleman worries about is that, to the end of his life, his name should remain uncommended."[1]

1. Which would mean that he has done nothing good.

15.21 The Master said: "The gentleman seeks it in himself; the small man seeks it in others."[1]

1. This chapter is closely related to the two previous ones in logical sequence: 15.19: The gentleman does not worry about men in high positions not knowing him; 15.20: But he does worry about the possibility that to the end of his life, people will have nothing good to say about him; 15.21: However, he does not blame others for his failure in life but turns inward to seek the cause of failure in himself. The two "its" stand for the cause of error or failure.

15.22 The Master said: "The gentleman is self-esteeming but not contentious, gregarious but not factious."[1]

1. Cf. 2.14.

15.23 The Master said: "The gentleman does not recommend a man on account of his sayings; he does not reject a man's sayings on account of the man."[1]

1. Cf. 14.4: ". . . but a man who possesses worthy sayings does not necessarily possess virtue." By the same token, one should not refuse to consider a man's good sayings because he is unvirtuous or of lowly station.

15.24 Zi-gong asked: "Is there one single word that one can practice throughout one's life?"

The Master said: "It is perhaps 'like-hearted considerateness.' 'What you do not wish for yourself, do not impose on others.' "[1]

1. Cf. 4.15, 5.12, 6.30, 12.2. Mark that "like-hearted considerateness" (*shu*) is one word in Chinese.

15.25 The Master said: "In associating with others, whom have I disparaged? Whom have I praised? If I have praised any, they are those who have been put to the test, the kind of people that made it possible for the Three Dynasties[1] to follow the straight path."

1. See 2.23, note 2.

15.26 The Master said: "I was in time to see blank spaces in character books and horse-owners seeking aid from another to break in a horse. Nowadays, there are no such people."[1]

1. When an official in charge of character correction in antiquity was preparing a character book and had doubts about the written form of a certain character, he would leave a blank space and wait for someone who knew how to write it to come along. (See 13.3.) When a horse-owner in ancient times could not break in a horse himself, he would ask someone else to do it for him. In commending the discretion and honesty of the ancients, the Master was censuring the pretension and hypocrisy of his contemporaries.

15.27 The Master said: "Sweet words undermine virtue; intolerance in small matters undermines great enterprises."

15.28 The Master said: "If the multitude loathes him, it must be looked into; if the multitude loves him, it must be looked into."[1]

1. Cf. 13.24.

15.29 The Master said: "It is the man[1] that can broaden the Way, not the Way that broadens the man."[2]

1. "Man" here stands for the emperor or the prince of a state.

2. That is, the Way of government becomes better with a ruler of higher cultivation and greater capacity and worse with one of lower cultivation and lesser capacity. The determining factor is the man and not the Way.

15.30 The Master said: "To make a mistake and not correct it is a mistake indeed!"

15.31 The Master said: "I once went the whole day without eating and the whole night without sleeping in order to think, but all fruitless. It would be better learning."[1]

    1. Cf. 2.15.

15.32 The Master said: "What the gentleman seeks is the Way and not food. If he farms, hunger lies therein; if he learns, an official's salary lies therein. What the gentleman worries about is the Way and not poverty."

15.33 The Master said: "If a man's wisdom is equal to it,[1] but his humanity cannot keep it, even if he has acquired it, he will surely lose it.[2] If his wisdom is equal to it and his humanity can keep it, but he does not preside over it with dignity, the people will not be reverent. If his wisdom is equal to it, his humanity can keep it, and he presides over it with dignity, but does not conduct it with the rituals, it is still not good."

    1. "It" refers throughout to the empire, or a state.

    2. The Master considered humanity the most important attainment for a sovereign, who must be able to embrace all the people with love. Without it, he would not be able to preserve the empire (or state) even if he has acquired it.

15.34 The Master said: "The gentleman may not be recognized for small skills but can undertake great responsibilities; the small man cannot undertake great responsibilities but may be recognized in small skills."

15.35　The Master said: "People need humanity more than water and fire. As for water and fire, I have seen people tread them and die, but I have never seen anyone die from treading humanity."

15.36　The Master said: "Confronting an act of humanity, do not yield the precedence even to your teacher."

15.37　The Master said: "The gentleman is firmly upright but not obstinately truthful."[1]

> 1. The gentleman is not always required to adhere to petty truthfulness in word and resoluteness in deed. He acts solely in conformity with righteousness. (Cf. 13.20, 14.17.)

15.38　The Master said: "In serving the sovereign, perform your duties reverently before taking your emolument."[1]

> 1. Cf. 6.22, 12.21.

15.39　The Master said: "I instruct regardless of kind."[1]

> 1. He does not discriminate on the basis of social class, position, natural endowment, or temperament. (Cf. 7.7.)

15.40　The Master said: "Those who pursue different ways[1] do not consult each other."

> 1. Referring to the different ethical and government theories of the Master's day.

15.41　The Master said: "As long as speech conveys the idea, it suffices."

15.42　Music Master Mian called. On reaching the steps, the Master said: "Here are the steps." On reaching his seat, the Master said: "Here is your seat." When all were seated, the Master told him: "So and so is here; so and so is there."

　　　　When Music Master Mian left, Zi-zhang asked: "Is this the way to talk to a music master?"

　　　　The Master said: "Yes, this is indeed the way to assist a music master."[1]

> 1. Note that music masters were always blind men in ancient China.

16.1 When Ji Shi[1] was about to attack Zhuan-yu,[2] Ran You and Ji-lu[3] called upon Master Kong, saying: "Ji Shi is about to take action against Zhuan-yu."

Master Kong said: "Qiu, are you not to blame for this?[4] Now, the lord of Zhuan-yu was long ago appointed by a former king[5] head administrator of sacrifices for Mount Dong Meng.[6] Besides, lying within the bounds of our territory, it is a vassal to the state. What reason do you have for attacking it?"

Ran You said: "His Excellency[7] wishes it. Neither of us, his two officers, wishes to do so."

Master Kong said: "Qiu, Zhou Ren[8] had a saying that goes: 'If you can contribute your ability, take your position; if you cannot, then stop.' When a man is in danger, you cannot support him; when he is falling, you cannot steady him. Then, why should he employ you as his aides? Moreover, what you said is mistaken indeed. When a tiger or a rhinoceros breaks loose from the cage, or a tortoise shell or a jade ornament is crushed in the cabinet, whose fault is it?"

Ran You said: "Now, Zhuan-yu is strongly fortified and is close to Bi.[9] If we do not take it today, it will surely become a source of concern to posterity."

Master Kong said: "Qiu, the gentleman loathes those who, instead of saying that they want something, always try to find an excuse for it. I hear that he who possesses a state or a noble house[10] does not worry about poverty but worries about unequal distribution.[11] He does not worry about scarcity[12] but worries about instability. For if there is equal distribution, there will be no poverty; if there is harmony, there will be no scarcity; if there is stability, there will be no downfall. In that case, if people in remote parts do not submit, he should then promote culture and virtue to make them come. And when they come, he should then make them live in peace. Now, you, Iou and Qiu, serve as His

Excellency's aides. But when people in remote parts do not submit, you cannot make them come; when the state is falling apart and splitting asunder, you cannot preserve it. Instead, you are planning to wield shield and spear within the state. I am afraid that Ji-sun's trouble does not lie in Zhuan-yu but lies within the awe-inspiring screen-wall."[13]

1. Referring to Ji Kang-zi.

2. A vassal state affiliated to Lu, 80 *li* northeast of what is now Bi County, Shandong Province. There is still a village bearing the named Zhuan-yu in that area today.

3. Both were serving Ji Kang-zi as house officers at the time.

4. As Ran was Ji Shi's chief house officer and helped Kang-zi to amass his wealth, the Master particularly suspected him of abetting Ji Shi in the attempt. (See 11.17.)

5. Referring to King Cheng of the Zhou Dynasty.

6. Also known as Mount Meng, situated 40 *li* south of what is now Mengyin, Shandong Province, bordering on Bi County to the southwest.

7. Referring to Ji Kang-zi.

8. A worthy historiographer of antiquity.

9. Ji Shi's fief, hence his concern about Zhuan-yu's potential menace to him and his descendants in the future. (See 6.9, note 3.)

10. I.e., a prince or a minister.

11. I.e., unequal distribution of wealth.

12. I.e., scarcity of population.

13. I.e., within the palace. In other words, Ji-sun's trouble lies with the prince of Lu, that is, Duke Ai.

16.2   Master Kong said: "When the empire possessed the Way, decrees governing the rituals, music, and punitive expeditions were issued by the Son of Heaven.[1] When the empire lost the Way, decrees governing the rituals, music, and punitive expeditions were issued by one of the various princes.[2] When they were issued by a prince, it is rare that in ten generations his family would not lose that prerogative. When they are issued by a minister, it is rare that in five generations, his family will not lose that prerogative. When a twofold officer[3] is in control of state decrees, it is rare that in three generations his family will not lose that prerogative. If the empire possessed the Way, state power would not be in the hands of ministers.[4] If the empire possessed the Way, the common people had nothing to censure."[5]

1. Such was the case during the reigns of the ancient sage kings.

2. Such was the case during the early days of the Spring and Autumn period.

3. I.e., a house officer, who was an officer to both the head of the noble house who employed him and the prince of the state.

4. Such was the case in Master Kong's day, i.e., the later part of the Spring and Autumn period, in which usurpation of state power by ministers and house officers was prevalent.

5. If the empire was well ruled, people had nothing to criticize.

16.3 Master Kong said: "The prerogative to confer official salaries has departed from the ducal house for five generations.[1] State power has reached the ministers for four generations.[2] Hence, the descendants of the Three Huans[3] are waning."[4]

1. The five generations include: Duke Xuan, Duke Cheng, Duke Xiang, Duke Zhao and Duke Ding of Lu. Master Kong's remarks were made in the initial stage of Duke Ding's reign.

2. The four generations include: Wen-zi, Wu-zi, Dao-zi, and Ping-zi of the Ji family.

3. So nicknamed because all three houses were descended from Duke Huan of Lu (r. 711–694 B.C.E.)

4. According to the Master's theory in 16.2, they were soon to lose their power.

16.4 Master Kong said: "Three types of friends are beneficial; three types of friends are harmful. To befriend the upright, befriend the truthful, and befriend the erudite is beneficial; to befriend the excessively respectful, befriend the obsequious, and befriend the glib-tongued is harmful."

16.5 Master Kong said: "Three types of delight are beneficial; three types of delight are harmful. To delight in conducting oneself in tune with the rituals and music,[1] delight in guiding people to goodness,[2] and delight in having many worthy friends is beneficial; to delight in extravagant pleasures, delight in idle loafing, and delight in the pleasure of feasting is harmful."

1. On ceremonial occasions, the gentleman was supposed to conform to the prescriptions of the rituals in appearance, deportment, speech, and manners and to follow the rhythm of music in movement.

2. A variant reading is: "delight in commending people's goodness."

16.6 Master Kong said: "Those who attend on the gentleman[1] are susceptible to three faults: to speak when not spoken to, which is called rashness; not to speak when spoken to, which is called concealing; to speak without first looking at his facial expression, which is called blindness."

    1. Referring to the sovereign.

16.7   Master Kong said: "The gentleman has three abstentions: in adolescence when his sap has not settled, he abstains from sex; in the prime of life when his sap is exuberant, he abstains from belligerence; in old age when his sap has waned, he abstains from greed."

16.8   Master Kong said: "The gentleman has three fears: he fears the decree of Heaven; he fears great men;[1] he fears the sage men's words. The small man, not knowing the decree of Heaven, does not fear it; he scorns great men and mocks the sage men's words."

    1. Referring to the emperor and the princes of the various states.

16.9   Master Kong said: "Those who know it[1] at birth belong to the highest category; those who know it through learning belong to the second category; those who learn it when baffled belong to the third category; those who do not learn even when baffled—such people belong to the lowest category."

    1. "It" stands for the Way here, i.e., humanity.

16.10   Master Kong said: "The gentleman has nine things to think about: In seeing, he thinks about clarity; in hearing, he thinks about distinctness; in facial expression, he thinks about gentleness; in appearance, he thinks about respectfulness; in speech, he thinks about wholehearted sincerity; in his duties, he thinks about reverence; in doubt, he thinks about inquiry; in anger, he thinks about its aftermath; on seeing gain, he thinks about righteousness."

16.11   Master Kong said: " 'On seeing a good man, I feel as if unable to catch up with someone. On seeing an evil man, I feel as if dipping my finger into boiling water.'[1] I have seen such men and heard such a saying. 'I live in seclusion to seek my aspiration; I perform my duty to implement the Way.'[2] I have heard such a saying but have never seen such a man."

1. The instinct of a man lagging behind in a race is to catch up with the one ahead of him, metaphorically, to catch up with the good man, of course; the impulse of a man dipping his finger into boiling water is, naturally, to pull it back instantly, metaphorically, to get away from the evil man at once. This quotation is believed to be an old saying.

2. "To seek my aspiration" implies "to seek the ancient sage kings' Way in the classics," and "perform my duty," "take office." This quotation is also believed to be an old saying.

16.12   Duke Jing of Qi[1] possessed a thousand teams of four horses each.[2] On the day of his death, people found no virtue to praise him with. Bo-yi and Shu-qi starved at the foot of Mount Shou-yang.[3] People to this day still praise them. This is perhaps what it means.[4]

1. See 12.11, note 1.

2. According to the rituals, the emperor was supposed to have 3,456 horses and the princes of the various states 1,296 each. Duke Jing's possession of 4,000 horses was a usurpation in violation of the rituals.

Note that this demonstrates the duke's military strength rather than his wealth. For "a thousand teams of four horses each" means one thousand war chariots.

3. Also known as Mount Lei-shou, its major peak being located to the northwest of the present-day Rei City, Shanxi Province.

4. That is, a ruler is praised for his virtue and not for his military strength. (Cf. 14.33.)

16.13   Chen Kang asked Bo-yu,[1] saying: "Have you heard anything different?"

Bo-yu replied, "I haven't. One day when Father was standing by himself, I hastened to cross the court.[2] He said: 'Have you learnt *Poetry*?' I replied: 'I haven't.' 'If you do not learn *Poetry*, you will not know how to speak.'[3] So I retired and learnt *Poetry*. Another day when he was again standing by himself, I hastened to cross the court. He said: 'Have you learnt *The Rituals*?' I replied: 'I haven't.' 'If you do not learn *The Rituals*, you have no way of establishing yourself.'[4] So I retired and learnt *The Rituals*. I have heard these two things."

Chen Kang retired and said joyfully: "I asked one question and obtained three answers: I heard about *Poetry*; I heard about *The Rituals*; I heard about how the gentleman keeps aloof from his son."[5]

1. Alias of Kong Li, Master Kong's son.

2. According to the rituals, when a subject walked by his sovereign or a son walked by his father, he was supposed to hasten his pace as a sign of reverence.

3. It was deemed necessary and proper for a gentleman to quote from *The Book of Poetry* in diplomatic dialogues and on other ceremonial occasions.

4. Cf. 8.8, 20.3.

5. That is, he was not partial to his son.

16.14 The wife of the sovereign of a state—the sovereign addresses her as "my lady" and her ladyship calls herself "your little lass";[1] the people of the state address her as "your sovereign ladyship"; to foreign states, she is referred to as "our deficient[2] junior sovereign"; people of foreign states also address her as "your sovereign ladyship."[3]

1. A modest way of referring herself to her lord, as if saying that she was not yet a fully grown-up person.

2. I.e., deficient in virtue. The emperor or the prince of a state in ancient China always modestly styled himself "we, the deficient one."

3. The presence of this chapter in *Lun Yu* is puzzling.

Book Seventeen

YANG HUO

17.1 Yang Huo[1] wished to see Master Kong, but Master Kong would not see him. So he presented Master Kong with a piglet. Master Kong, availing himself of the other's absence, went to return his respects[2] but met him on the way.

He said to Master Kong: "Come, I want to speak with you." Then he added: "To pocket one's gem and allow one's state to go awry[3]—can this be called humanity? I'd say: 'It cannot.' To love to engage in state affairs but to have repeatedly missed the opportunity—can this be called wisdom? I'd say: 'It cannot.' The days and moons are flitting away; the years do not us await."

Master Kong said: "All right, I shall take office."[4]

1. Also known as Yang Hu, originally chief house officer of the noble house of Ji-sun. Later, he usurped state power and was the most influential minister in court at this juncture.

2. Master Kong, who was a *shi* at the time, was obliged by the rituals to return his respects to Yang but was careful to do so when Yang was not at home.

3. "To pocket one's gem" alludes to Master Kong's not taking office, and "to allow one's state to go awry," to his seeing the state in disorder but not doing anything about it.

4. A perfunctory answer to avoid further ado. Instead, the Master devoted himself to editing and teaching the classics.

17.2 The Master said: "By nature, people are close to one another; through practice, they drift far apart."[1]

The Master said: "Only the highest of the wise and the lowest of the stupid do not change."[2]

1. Human nature is neutral at birth. Goodness and evil are acquired in later life, owing to the environments in which people are brought up and the company they keep.

2. "The highest of the wise" refers to "those who know it at birth," i.e.,

the sages; "the lowest of the stupid," to "those who do not learn even when baffled," i.e., the depraved and incorrigible. (See 16.9.)

17.3   When the Master went to Wu City,[1] he heard the sounds of stringed instruments and chanting.[2] The Master, with a gentle smile, said: "In killing a chicken, why need you use an ox-knife?"[3]

Zi-you replied: "Formerly I heard Master say: 'If the gentleman acquires the Way, he loves men; if the small man acquires the Way, he is easy to command.' "[4]

The Master said: "Gentlemen, what Yan[5] said is correct. My previous remark was but a joke."

1. See 6.14, note 1.

2. I.e., chanting poems from *The Book of Poetry* to the accompaniment of stringed instruments, which means that the people at Wu City were being instructed in the rituals and music.

3. A metaphor signifying that in governing a small county, there was no need to teach the rituals and music.

4. "The gentleman" here represents children of the nobility, and "the small man," those of the commoners.

5. Zi-you's given name.

17.4   Gong-shan Fu-rao, using Bi as his base, staged a revolt. When he summoned, the Master was inclined to go.[1]

Zi-lu, displeased, said: "If we have nowhere to go, let us stop trying. Why must we go to Gong-shan Shi's place?"

The Master said: "He who summoned me—could he have done so for no purpose?[2] If anyone should employ me again, I would create an eastern Zhou!"[3]

1. During the Spring and Autumn period, usurpations and rebellions abounded. Gong-shan Fu-rao, then magistrate of Ji-sun's fief Bi County, revolted with Yang Huo, taking Ji Huan-zi, then head of the Ji house, into custody and proclaiming that they would strengthen the ducal house of Lu and repress Ji-sun (himself a usurper of state power). This sounded to the Master like a righteous cause; hence his inclination to join Gong-shan.

2. That is, he certainly wanted to employ me.

3. I.e., I would create a Zhou kind of government in the East. Lu was East, and Zhou West. Hence, an eastern Zhou. Owing to Zi-lu's objection and Gong-shan's attack on the ducal house, the Master did not go in the end.

17.5 When Zi-zhang asked Master Kong about humanity, Master Kong said: "To be able to practice five things under Heaven constitutes humanity."

When further questioned about them, he said: "Respectfulness, lenience, truthfulness, industry, and beneficence. Be respectful and you shall not be humiliated; be lenient and you shall win the multitude; be truthful and the people shall trust you; be industrious and you shall score successes; be beneficent and you shall be fit to employ the people."

17.6 When Bi Xi[1] summoned, the Master was inclined to go.

Zi-lu said: "Formerly, I heard Master say: 'If a man personally engages in evil-doing, the gentleman does not enter his state.' Now Bi Xi, with Zhong-mou[2] as his base, has staged a revolt. Sir, your going there—how do you justify it?"

The Master said: "Yes, I did make such a remark. However, did I not also say: 'That which is hard enough can stand grinding without becoming thinner?' Did I not also say: 'That which is white enough can stand dyeing in a dark fluid without turning black'?[3] I am not a gourd, am I? How could I be hung up somewhere without eating?"[4]

1. Magistrate of Zhong-mou, fief of Zhao Jian-zi, the most influential minister in the State of Jin at the time.

2. A county of Jin, situated between what is now Xing-tai and Han-dan in Hebei Province.

3. These are believed to be proverbs of the time. Both are metaphors signifying that a man of integrity will remain pure and untainted in sordid circumstances.

4. That is to say, I have to seek an office and earn my living.

17.7 The Master said: "Iou, have you heard 'the six words and their six latent defects'?"[1]

Zi-lu replied: "I haven't."

"Be seated.[2] Let me explain to you. To love humanity and not to love learning—the latent defect is foolishness;[3] to love wisdom and not to love learning—the latent defect is unprincipledness;[4] to love truthfulness and not to love learning—the latent defect is harmfulness;[5] to love straightforwardness and not to love learning—the latent defect is impetuosity;[6] to love courage and not to love learning—the latent defect is rebelliousness; to love staunchness and not to love learning—the latent defect is recklessness."

1. This is believed to be an ancient catch phrase. The six words represent the six virtues that follow, namely, humanity, wisdom, truthfulness, straightforwardness, courage, and staunchness.

2. Zi-lu having risen to answer the question, the Master told him to sit down.

3. Foolishness implies being easily trapped or duped. Note that learning here refers to acquiring the rituals.

4. If a wise man is not guided by the rituals, he will do whatever he likes, neither adhering to righteousness nor relying on humanity; hence his lack of principle.

5. If a truthful man is not guided by the rituals, he knows only the necessity of keeping promises without being able to judge whether a promise is right or wrong; hence the latent harm.

6. If a straightforward man is not guided by the rituals, he will be too harsh in criticizing people's faults and thus hurt their feelings. (Cf. 8.2.)

17.8 The Master said: "Young men, why do you not learn *Poetry? Poetry* can be of help to you in using metaphors, observing things, becoming gregarious, employing satire, serving your father nearby, serving your sovereign afar, and making you better acquainted with the names of birds, beasts, grasses, and trees."[1]

1. Cf. 17.9

17.9 The Master said to Bo-yu: "Have you learnt *South of Zhou* and *South of Shao?*[1] If a man does not learn *South of Zhou* and *South of Shao*, he is like one standing with his face against the wall."[2]

1. Titles of the first two sections of *The Book of Poetry, Ballads of the Various States.*

2. I.e., unable to see anything clearly. (Cf. 17.8.)

17.10 The Master said: " 'The rituals, the rituals,' they say. Do they merely refer to jade and silk?[1] 'Music, music,' they say.[2] Do they merely refer to bells and drums?"

1. The essence of the rituals lies in restraining people's actions, thus bringing peace to the sovereign and order to the people, whereas jade and silk (used as gifts) were only instrumental to creating reverence.

2. The essence of music lies in harmonizing people's feelings thus trans-

forming conventions and changing customs, whereas bells and drums were only instrumental to creating harmony.

Note that "they" here stands for the ancient sage kings.

17.11   The Master said: "He who is awesome of mien but faint of heart, to cite an example from small men, is perhaps like a hole-boring and wall-climbing burglar?"[1]

> 1. The Master was satirizing those who came by the name of righteousness through deception and who were always in fear of being found out.

17.12   The Master said: "The 'honest men'[1] of your prefecture undermine virtue."

> 1. The Master was censuring the hypocrites of the prefectures who seem to be sincere and truthful in word, pure and clean in deed, but who wallow in the mire with the evil people of the world. (Cf. 12.20, 17.11.)

17.13   The Master said: "To hear something in the street and discourse on it along the road is to forsake virtue."[1]

> 1. A true scholar should learn more about the Way to strengthen his virtue, not to brag about it to others. To learn something in the street and discourse on it to others there and then is not strengthening one's virtue but abandoning it. (Cf. 14.24.)

17.14   The Master said: "Can a vulgar fellow serve the sovereign? When he has not obtained it,[1] he worries about obtaining it.[2] Having obtained it, he worries about losing it. When he worries about losing it, he will stop at nothing."

> 1. Referring to an official position.
> 2. This should read: "he worries about *not* obtaining it."

17.15   The Master said: "In antiquity, people had three infirmities. Today, even these are nowhere to be found.[1] In antiquity, the high-minded were unreserved; today, the high-minded are unprincipled. In antiquity, the self-esteeming were clean and honest; today, the self-esteeming are irritable and perverse. In antiquity, the foolish were straightforward; today, the foolish are utterly deceitful."

1. That is, even the defects of the ancients were better than those of his contemporaries.

17.16   The Master said: "Sweet words and a pleasing countenance have indeed little humanity in them!"[1]

1. Cf. 1.3, 5.25.

17.17   The Master said: "I loathe purple usurping the place of red;[1] I loathe the songs of Zheng[2] confounding classical music; I loathe the glib-tongued toppling states and noble houses."

1. Red was the orthodox color for official robes in the Zhou Dynasty, whereas purple was an unorthodox mixed color that was in vogue during the Spring and Autumn period.
2. See 15.11.

17.18   The Master said: "I wish to speak no more."
Zi-gong said: "Sir, if you do not speak, what shall we, your pupils, abide by?"
The Master said: "What does Heaven say? Yet the four seasons revolve and a hundred things grow. What does Heaven say?"[1]

1. This chapter strongly suggests the influence of Lao Zi, the Taoist philosopher. In the *Dao De Jing*, Lao Zi repeatedly advocates "speechless instruction," with few laws and decrees and little verbal instruction on the part of the ruler. Everything is allowed to take its own course as the Dao (the law of nature) does. (Cf. the *Dao De Jing*, e.g., Chs. 2, 43.)

17.19   Ru Bei[1] wished to see Master Kong, but Master Kong declined on the excuse of illness. As soon as the go-between[2] went out of the door, he took his zither and sang to it so that the former might hear him.[3]

1. One of the Master's major disciples. This episode must have taken place before Ru Bei enrolled at the Master's school.
2. See 14.44, note 2.
3. Despite endless speculation about this incident, the Master's reason for behaving this way remains a puzzle to us.

17.20   Zai Wo asked about the three-year mourning,[1] saying: "A twelve-month is already long enough. 'If the gentleman for three years does not perform the rituals, the rituals will surely decline; if for

three years he does not perform music, music will surely fall apart.'
The old grains will have been consumed, the new grains will have
ripened, and the different kinds of fire-drilling wood will have com-
pleted their cycle.² A twelvemonth is good enough."

The Master said: "Eating rice and wearing brocade³—do you
feel at ease?"

Zai Wo said: "I do."

"If you do, then do so! When the gentleman is in mourning:
eating delicacies, he does not relish their good taste; listening to
music, he does not feel any happiness; living at home, he does not
enjoy its comfort.⁴ Therefore, he does not do so. Now, if you feel
at ease, do so!"

When Zai Wo went out, the Master said: "How inhumane Yu⁵
is! A son does not leave his parents' arms until three years after his
birth. The three-year mourning is a universal mourning under
Heaven. Does Yu have three years' love for his parents?"

1. The longest of mourning terms, observed by sons at the death of a parent,
by princes of the various states at the death of the emperor, and by the subjects
of a state at the death of its reigning prince.

2. In ancient China, people made fire by drilling into wood. The wood used
for this purpose varied with each season.

3. Rice was a delicacy in North China in those days.

4. According to the rituals, a bereaved son was supposed to live in a thatched
hut built for the three-year mourning term instead of living at home as usual.

5. Zai Wo's given name.

17.21 The Master said: "Those who are sated with food all day without
applying their minds to anything at all are difficult indeed!¹ Are
there no people who play double six and siege?² Even doing these
would be better than to stop thinking altogether."

1. I.e., difficult to instruct in the Way.

2. "Double six" is a board game for two, so-called because each side has six
pieces. *Yi* refers to the Chinese board game *weiqi* (literally, "siege"), or the
Japanese *go*. (Cf. 15.17.)

17.22 Zi-lu said: "Does the gentleman uphold courage?"

The Master said: "The gentleman regards righteousness as supreme. A gentleman who possesses courage but wants righteousness will become a rebel; a small man who possesses courage but wants righteousness will become a bandit."[1]

1. The gentleman and the small man here are differentiated by rank.

17.23 Zi-gong said: "Does the gentleman also have people he loathes?"

The Master said: "Yes, I do. I loathe those who babble about other people's vices; I loathe those who, being in the lower stream, slander their superiors; I loathe those who are courageous but have no regard for the rituals; I loathe those who are resolute and daring but stubborn."

Then he said: "Ci, are there also people you loathe?"

"I loathe those who plagiarize and consider themselves wise; I loathe those who are impertinent and consider themselves courageous; I loathe those who divulge other people's unseemly secrets and consider themselves straightforward."

17.24 The Master said: "Women and small men[1] are the most difficult to keep: If you stay close to them, they become insolent; if you keep them at a distance, they are resentful."[2]

1. "Women" here refers to concubines and maid servants and "small men," to men servants, including eunuchs.

2. This was an admonition for those who possessed a state or a noble house. To treat concubines and servants properly formed an inseparable part of good household management for the nobility.

17.25 The Master said: "If, at forty, a man is still loathed, he is done for."

Book Eighteen

WEI ZI *(The Viscount of Wei)*

18.1   The viscount of Wei left him; the viscount of Ji became his slave; Bi Gan remonstrated and was killed.[1]

    Master Kong said: "The Yin had three men of humanity."[2]

> 1. These three men all served the notorious tyrant King Zhou of Yin. (See 19.20, note 1.) The first was his half brother; the second and third were his uncles. When King Wu of Zhou conquered the tyrant Zhou, he granted the viscount of Wei the land of Song, and the viscount of Ji the land of Korea.
>
> 2. Because of their love for the people and the empire, they were among the handful of historical figures praised by the Master as men of humanity.

18.2   When Liu-xia Hui[1] served as criminal judge, he was thrice dismissed. Someone said: "Sir, can you not leave?"

    He said: "If I pursue the straight way in serving man, where can I go without being thrice dismissed? If I pursue the crooked way in serving man, why must I leave my father and mother's state?"[1]

> 1. See 15.14, 18.8.

18.3   Duke Jing of Qi, on how to treat Master Kong, said: "To treat him like Ji Shi—that we cannot do. We shall treat him like someone between Ji and Meng."[1]

    The duke said: "We are too old to employ him now."[2] Whereupon, Master Kong departed.

> 1. Admiring the sage's great accomplishments in virtue and the rituals, the duke was inclined to employ him. He decided to pay the Master a salary between that of Prime Minister Ji-sun and that of Meng-sun, who was minister of military affairs. Ji and Meng were two of the three noble lords in control of Lu's state affairs, the other being Zhong. (See 3.2, note 1.)
>
> 2. This remark was evidently made on a later occasion.

18.4 When the man of Qi¹ presented a group of singing girls, Ji Huan-zi²
accepted them. For three days, there was no court. Master Kong
departed.³

> 1. Referring to Duke Jing of Qi.
> 2. This incident took place in the 14th year of Duke Ding's reign (496
> B.C.E.), when Master Kong was serving as his minister of justice and had
> achieved great accomplishments in government. The apparent purpose of this
> gift was to corrupt Duke Ding and his prime minister, Ji Huan-zi, and to defeat
> the Master's plans to reform the State of Lu.
> 3. Posthumous title of Ji-sun Si (?–492 B.C.E.), then head of the Ji-sun house
> and prime minister of Lu.

18.5 Chu's Madman Jie-yu¹ passed by Master Kong, singing:

> "O phoenix! O phoenix!
> How thy virtue hath declined!
> What hath gone by is beyond remonstration;
> What is to come may yet be overtaken.
> Stay! Stay!
> Perilous are those engaged in government today."²

Master Kong descended, hoping to speak with him, but he hastened off to evade him. So the Master did not get to speak with
him.

> 1. Alias of Lu Tong, a hermit of Chu. During the reign of King Zhao of
> Chu, government being erratic, he feigned lunacy, refusing to take office. Hence
> the nickname "Chu's Madman."
> 2. Jie-yu, knowing well of Master Kong's great moral accomplishments,
> compared him to the divine bird phoenix. (See 9.9, note 1.) In figurative lan-
> guage, he advised the Master to stop seeking office and retire from the chaotic
> world.

18.6 Chang-ju and Jie-ni were sowing side by side. Master Kong, passing
by, sent Zi-lu to inquire where the ford was.
Chang-ju said: "Who is the man holding the reins?"
Zi-lu said: "It is Kong Qiu."
Chang-ju said: "Is it the Kong Qiu of Lu?"
Zi-lu said: "Yes."
Chang-ju said: "Then he knows where the ford is."¹
Thereupon, Zi-lu asked of Jie-ni.
Jie-ni said: "Who are you, sir?"

Zi-lu said: "I am one Zhong Iou."

Jie-ni said: "Are you a disciple of Lu's Kong Qiu?"

Zi-lu replied: "Yes."

Jie-ni said: "Turbulent waves are surging everywhere under Heaven. With whom[2] are you to change all this? Besides, would it not be better for you to follow a *shi* who fled the world[3] than one who fled a man?"[4] And he went on covering the seeds without stopping.

Zi-lu departed and reported it. The Master, disappointed, said: "I cannot herd with birds and beasts, can I? If I do not associate with my fellow men, with whom shall I associate then? If the empire possessed the Way, I would not be involved in changing it."

1. This remark implies sarcastically that as the Master had been traveling around the empire so much, he certainly knew where the ford was.

2. Which of the various princes in the epoch.

3. Jie-ni himself, who had fled the world altogether.

4. Master Kong, who had only fled the Prince of Lu and was seeking another to employ him. (See 14.37.)

18.7 Zi-lu, who had been following, fell behind. On encountering an old man carrying a weeding implement on his shoulder with a staff, Zi-lu asked: "Sir, did you see my master?"

The old man said: "Your four limbs seem unused to regular toil, and you look incapable of distinguishing the five grains. Who may your master be?" Leaning on his staff, he fell to weeding.[1] Zi-lu, cupping his hands, stood by.

The old man persuaded Zi-lu to stay for the night. Having killed a chicken and steamed some millet, he fed him and introduced him to his two sons.

The next day, Zi-lu departed and reported it. The Master said: "It must be a hermit." He then sent Zi-lu back to see him. But upon his arrival, the old man had already left.

Zi-lu said: "Not to take office is to ignore one's duty. Since the etiquette between the old and the young cannot be abandoned, how, then, can the duty between the sovereign and the subject be abandoned? In attempting to preserve one's own purity, one undermines an important moral principle. The gentleman, in taking office, is performing his duty. That the Way shall not prevail, he already knows."[2]

1. In the rice paddies of China, the farmers weed with one foot leaning on a staff to support themselves.

2. "The gentleman" here refers to Master Kong.

18.8 Lofty hermits were: Bo-yi, Shu-qi, Yu-zhong, Yi-yi, Zhu-zhang, Liu-xia Hui, and Shao-lian.[1]

The Master said: "The ones that neither abated their aspirations nor brought disgrace upon themselves were perhaps Bo-yi and Shu-qi."[2]

He said about Liu-xia Hui and Shao-lian: "They did abate their aspirations and bring disgrace upon themselves. However, their speech conformed to moral principle and their conduct conformed to deliberation, that is all."[3]

He said about Yu-zhong and Yi-yi: "They lived in seclusion and abandoned speech.[4] Their character conformed to purity and their self-banishment conformed to expediency.[5] However, I am different from them. I have neither favorable nor unfavorable situation."[6]

1. Of the seven men mentioned, not much is known about Yu-zhong, Yi-yi, Zhu-zhang, and Shao-lian.

2. Bo-yi and Shu-qi fled the world and starved to death; therefore, they did not abate their aspirations. They refused to take office in the court of the Zhou Dynasty; therefore, they did not bring disgrace upon themselves.

3. Both men served in the court of Lu during a chaotic period, and the former was dismissed three times. So they did abate their aspirations and bring disgrace upon themselves. But they always measured their speech and action carefully with righteousness.

4. I.e., they gave up criticizing government measures.

5. I.e., their fleeing the world in a chaotic epoch conformed to the doctrine of expediency (see Terms, pp. 26–28).

6. I.e., he was neither bent on advancing nor on retreating but acted in conformity with what was righteous.

18.9 Senior Music Master Zhi left for Qi; Second Repast[1] Gan left for Chu; Third Repast Liao left for Cai; Fourth Repast Que left for Qin;[2] Drummer Fang-shu went into the River area;[3] Hand-drummer Wu went into the River Han area;[4] Junior Music Master Yang and Chime-stone player Xiang went to sea.

1. Official title of Gan, court musician of Lu, whose duty it was to entertain the prince with music at the second meal each day. (It may be inferred that Senior Music Master Zhi was responsible for music at the first repast.) As the

prince of Lu lost the Way, the court musicians all left Lu and scattered in various directions.

2. A large state in the present-day Shaanxi Province.

3. That part of the present-day Henan Province that lies to the north of the Yellow River.

4. The area extending from the southern part of the present-day Shaanxi Province to the north bank of River Han, which rises in Shaanxi Province and flows through Shaanxi and Hubei provinces into the Yangtze River.

18.10 The Duke of Zhou said to the Duke of Lu:[1] "The gentleman[2] does not neglect his kin or give his great ministers cause to complain that their advices are not adopted. His old acquaintances,[3] except for major offences, he does not abandon. He does not demand perfection in one man."[4]

1. Bo-qin, eldest son to Duke Dan of Zhou, first prince of Lu (r. 1115? B.C.E.–?).

2. The prince of a state.

3. His former schoolmates when he was crown prince.

4. These were Duke Dan's exhortations for his son Bo-qin when the latter was about to leave Hao-jing, the capital of the Western Zhou Dynasty, to assume office as the First Duke of Lu.

18.11 The Zhou had eight *shi*: Bo-da, Bo-kuo, Zhong-tu, Zhong-hu, Shu-ye, Shu-xia, Ji-sui, and Ji-qua.[1]

1. These eight men are believed to be four sets of twins born of the same mother early in the Zhou Dynasty. All eight served as distinguished courtiers; hence the record of their names.

19.1 Zi-zhang said: "A *shi* who, on seeing danger, is ready to give his life; on seeing gain, thinks of righteousness; in offering sacrifices, thinks of reverence; in mourning, thinks of grief, is commendable indeed!"

19.2 Zi-zhang said: "He who neither adheres to virtue tenaciously nor believes in the Way firmly—how can we say there is such a man? How can we say there is no such man?"[1]

> 1. That is, his existence does not carry much weight to the world.

19.3 When one of Zi-xia's pupils asked Zi-zhang about making friends, Zi-zhang said: "What did Zi-xia say?"

The pupil replied: "Zi-xia said: 'Those who are good enough— associate with them; those who are not good enough—reject them.' "[1]

Zi-zhang said: "This is different from what I have heard: 'The gentleman esteems the worthy and tolerates the multitude; he commends the good and sympathizes with those who are incapable.' If I am eminently worthy, what men can I not tolerate? If I am unworthy, others will reject me. How can I reject others?"[2]

> 1. Zi-xia was transmitting the Master's teaching: "... and (a gentleman) does not befriend those beneath him" (1.8).
> 2. Zi-zhang was transmitting the Master's teaching: "... they should love all the multitude and keep close to humane men" (cf. 1.6).

19.4 Zi-xia said: "Even minor ways[1] must have something worth seeing. However, journeying afar, one might get bogged down.[2] Hence, the gentleman does not pursue them."

> 1. Referring to the theories of the various schools other than that of the Ru (Confucian) School. (Cf. 2.16.)

2. A metaphor signifying that the other theories might become handicaps to those who were pursuing the Way of humanity.

19.5 Zi-xia said: "He who each day acquires something he lacks and each moon does not forget what he is proficient in may be said to love learning indeed."[1]

> 1. Cf. 2.11.

19.6 Zi-xia said: "To learn extensively and memorize tenaciously;[1] to inquire specifically and think closely[2]—humanity lies therein."[3]

> 1. A variant reading of this phrase is: "To learn extensively and adhere to your aspirations firmly; . . ."
>
> 2. To inquire about what one has not understood thoroughly and think about what is within one's reach to practice.
>
> 3. If one can devote oneself to acquiring the Way with such dedication, although one has not reached humanity yet, one has at least made it possible to practice it.

19.7 Zi-xia said: "The hundred artisans[1] live in the shop to perfect their craftsmanship; the gentleman engages in learning to exhaust the Way."[2]

> 1. "The hundred artisans" here means artisans of all trades.
>
> 2. A variant reading says: "the gentleman lives at school to exhaust the Way."

19.8 Zi-xia said: "When the small man makes a mistake, he always glosses over it."

19.9 The gentleman[1] has three changes: when gazed at, he looks awesome; when approached, he is gentle; when listened to, he sounds austere.[2]

> 1. Referring to Master Kong.
>
> 2. Cf. 7.37.

19.10 Zi-xia said: "The gentleman[1] must be trusted before making the people toil. If he is not trusted, they will consider themselves tyrannized. He must be trusted before remonstrating. If he is not trusted, the sovereign will consider himself slandered."

> 1. Referring to a consul or a minister.

19.11   Zi-xia said: "In major virtues,[1] one may not overstep the threshold; in minor virtues,[2] some leeway is permissible."

>   1. Referring to such virtues as filial piety and brotherly obedience.
>   2. Referring to such virtues as dignity in appearance and respectfulness in manner.

19.12   Zi-you said: "Zi-xia's students and pupils, in coping with such duties as sprinkling and sweeping, responding and answering, advancing and retreating,[1] are good enough. However, these are the incidentals. As for the fundamentals, they have none. What can one do with them?"[2]

Zi-xia, on hearing this, said: "Alas! Yan You[3] is mistaken indeed! Of the gentleman's Way,[4] which part is to be transmitted first; which part is to be ignored in the end? Like herbs and trees, they should be divided into different categories.[5] The gentleman's Way—how can it be mishandled? However, the only one who could carry it from beginning to end systematically was perhaps the sage man."[6]

>   1. All these have to do with such matters as reception of guests, ceremonial preparations, and performance of the rituals.
>   2. Zi-you was criticizing Zi-xia for teaching his pupils the small details and ignoring the major principles of the rituals and music.
>   3. Zi-you, whose full name was Yan Yan, was also known as Yan You.
>   4. Referring to the rituals and music here, major requirements in self-cultivation and statecraft.
>   5. A simile signifying that the major principles and minor principles of the Way ought to be arranged in proper order and taught systematically.
>   6. Refering to Master Kong.

19.13   Zi-xia said: "Those who excel in office should learn;[1] those who excel in learning should take office."[2]

>   1. In those days, children of the nobility inherited titles and official positions from their fathers or elder brothers without having to go to school first. If they were able to discharge their duties well enough, they should go to school to learn the rituals and music and become better officials. (Cf. 11.1, note 2.)
>   2. The very aim of acquiring the rituals and music at Master Kong's school was to take office and implement the sage kings' Way of humane government.
>   Variant readings of this chapter are: "Those who have energy to spare after conducting state affairs should learn; those who have energy to spare after learning should take office" and, "Those who have energy to spare after conducting state affairs should learn; those who excel in learning should take office."

19.14 Zi-you said: "In mourning, one should stop after exhausting one's grief."[1]

> 1. This has to do with mourning for one's parents. (Cf. 19.17.)

19.15 Zi-you said: "My friend Zhang[1] is difficult to emulate.[2] However, he has not attained humanity yet."

> 1. Short for Zi-zhang.
> 2. This was said of Zi-zhang's appearance and manners, which formed part of the gentleman's cultivation in the rituals but not its essence. (Cf. 19.16.)

19.16 Master Zeng said: "How impressive Zhang looks! However, it is difficult to pursue humanity with him."[1]

> 1. Cf. 19.15.

19.17 Master Zeng said: "I heard it from the Master: 'There is hardly anything that can make a man spontaneously exhaust his grief. If an exception must be made, it is perhaps a parent's death.' "[1]

> 1. Cf. 19.14.

19.18 Master Zeng said: "I heard it from the Master: 'Of Meng Zhuang-zi's[1] filial piety, other aspects are possible to emulate, but the way he never replaced his father's officers and his father's decrees is difficult to emulate.' "

> 1. Minister of Lu, son to Meng Xian-zi. (Cf. 1.11, 4.20.)

19.19 When Meng Shi[1] appointed Yang Fu[2] criminal judge, the latter consulted Master Zeng.
Master Zeng said: "Since the sovereign lost the Way, the people have long gone astray. If you get at the truth of a case, have compassion, and do not take delight in it."

> 1. Head of the noble house of Meng-sun. The identity of this man is untraceable.
> 2. One of Master Zeng's pupils. Little is known about him.

19.20 Zi-gong said: "Zhou's[1] wickedness was hardly as monstrous as that. Hence, the gentleman loathes to find himself in the lower stream, for all the evils under Heaven flow thither."

1. Posthumous title of Shou-xin, last emperor of the Yin (or Shang) Dynasty (r. 1099?–1066? B.C.E.), the most notorious tyrant in Chinese history, known for his wanton brutality and licentiousness. Many of his ministers who remonstrated against his tyranny were killed by him, including his uncle Bi Gan. (See 18.1.) After being defeated in a revolution led by Ji Chang, who later became King Wu of the Zhou Dynasty, he burned himself to death, thus ending the Yin Dynasty.

19.21 Zi-gong said: "The gentleman's errors are like the eclipses of the sun and the moon. When he makes one, everyone sees it; when he corrects it, everyone looks up to him."

19.22 Wei's Gong-sun Chao asked of Zi-gong: "From whom did Zhong-ni[1] learn?"

Zi-gong said: "The Way of Wen and Wu[2] had not crumbled to the ground. It was still there among men. The worthy remembered its major tenets; the unworthy remembered its minor tenets. None did not possess a portion of the Way of Wen and Wu. From whom did the Master not learn? And yet what regular teachers did he have?"

1. Master Kong's alias.
2. For King Wen and King Wu, see 9.5, note 2, and 8.20, note 1. Both were ancient sage kings greatly admired by Master Kong.

19.23 Shu-sun Wu-shu[1] spoke to the ministers at court, saying: "Zi-gong[2] is worthier than Zhong-ni."

When Zi-fu Jing-bo[3] told Zi-gong about it, Zi-gong said: "Take our enclosing walls as an example. My wall is shoulder-high, over which one may peep at the comeliness of my residential quarters. The Master's wall is several ren[4] high. If one cannot find the gate to enter, one will see neither the beauty of his ancestral temple nor the splendor of a hundred official buildings. Those who can find the gate are perhaps few. That His Excellency should have made such a remark—is it not natural enough?"

1. Minister of Lu, a member of the house of Shu-sun, one of the three noble houses that controlled state power in Lu.

2. Well accomplished in speech, Zi-gong was one of Master Kong's prominent disciples. He first distinguished himself in diplomacy and eventually became an influential figure in interstate affairs. Subsequently, he served as prime minister in Lu and then in Wei. His achievements in government were truly admirable. That is perhaps why both Shu-sun Wu-shu and Chen Zi-qin (19.25) suspected that he was worthier than his master.

3. One of Master Kong's major disciples.

4. A linear measure approximately equivalent to eight feet. (Some say seven feet.)

19.24 When Shu-sun Wu-shu slandered Zhong-ni, Zi-gong said: "It is useless to do so. Zhong-ni is above slander. Other men of worth are mounds and hillocks, which may yet be surmounted. Zhong-ni is the sun and the moon, which can never be surmounted. Although men may wish to sever themselves,[1] what harm will it do to the sun and the moon? It only shows that they do not know their capacity."

1. I.e., from the sun and the moon.

19.25 Chen Zi-qin[1] said to Zi-gong: "Sir, you are being modest. How can Zhong-ni be worthier than you?"

Zi-gong said: "The gentleman, for one single remark, may be considered wise and, for one single remark, may be considered unwise. One cannot be indiscreet in speech. For the impossibility of equaling the Master is like the impossibility of ascending Heaven by scaling a ladder. If the Master had acquired a state or a fief, it would have been just like what people used to say: 'When he set forth to establish them,[3] they would forthwith follow; when he set forth to pacify them,[3] they would forthwith follow; when he set forth to pacify them,[4] they would forthwith flock to him; when he set forth to mobilize them, they would rothwith respond. When he lived, he was honored; when he died, he was lamented.' How could he ever be equaled?"

1. One of Master Kong's Major Disciples.

2. That is, to establish the people on the rituals. (Cf. 8.8, 16.13, 20.3.)

3. That is, to guide them with virtue. (Cf. 2.3.)

4. That is, to pacify those in remote parts by promoting culture and virtue. (Cf. 16.1.)

Book Twenty

YAO YUE *(Yao Said)*

20.1 Yao[1] said:

"Hail, thou Shun![2]
Heaven's order of evolution rests upon thy person.[3]
Faithfully adhere to the mean
And thy rule shall extend to the Four Seas' ends;[4]
Heaven's blessings shall last throughout thy reign."[5]

Shun issued the same decree to Yu.[6]
(Tang[7]) said:

"We, thy little son[8] Lü, venture to use a black bull,[9]
And venture to clearly report to thee,
Thou great sovereign of Heaven:
'Those who have sinned, we dare not pardon;
Thy subject,[10] we dare not cover up.
For all this is discerned in thy heart.
If we ourself have sinned,
Do not implicate the ten thousand states;[11]
If the ten thousand states have sinned,
Let the sin rest on our person.' "[12]

The Zhou, being richly endowed, abounded in good men.[13]

"Although he[14] has close kinsmen,
They cannot match our humane men.
If the hundred family names should transgress,
Let the blame rest on us one person."[15]

"Be strict with weight and capacity measures, be meticulous with musical temperament and linear measures, rehabilitate neglected offices, and government decrees shall prevail in the various states.

"Revive defunct states, restore extinct noble houses,[16] promote lofty recluses,[17] and all under Heaven shall turn their hearts to you.

"Special importance should be attached to: the people, food, mourning, and sacrifice.

"Be lenient and you shall win the multitude; be truthful and the people shall trust you; be industrious and you shall score successes; be impartial and the people shall be pleased."[18]

1. See 6.30, note 1.

2. See 6.30, note 2.

3. His son Dan-zhu being unworthy, Yao yielded the throne to his minister Shun, who had been his regent for 30 years.

4. See 12.5, note 3.

5. Yao issued this decree to Shun on the occasion of yielding the throne to the latter.

A variant reading of the last two lines is:
"If the Four Seas should be reduced to privation,
Heaven's blessings would end forever."

6. His son Shang-jun being unworthy, Shun yielded the throne to his minister Yu, who tamed the Yellow River for him.

7. The founding father of the Shang Dynasty.
(See 12.22, note 2.)

8. In ancient China, the emperor regarded Heaven as his father, Earth as his mother, and himself as the Son of Heaven.

9. I.e., in sacrifice. The Yin Dynasty upheld the white color, whereas the Xia Dynasty upheld the black color. However, at this juncture, the Yin had not changed the rituals of the Xia yet. Hence, Tang still used a black bull in a sacrificial ceremony.

10. The tyrant Jie, last king of the Xia Dynasty.

11. Referring to people of all the states in the empire.

12. This was Tang's prayer for rain in a big drought.

13. King Wu of Zhou had 10 competent ministers. (Cf. 8.20.)

14. The tyrant Zhou, last king of the Yin Dynasty.

15. This was King Wu of Zhou's pledge to the army and those princes of the various states who supported his punitive expedition against Zhou before going off to war.

16. States and noble houses that had been unjustly exterminated by former kings.

17. Worthy men of the previous dynasty who had fled the new regime to live in seclusion.

18. The last four paragraphs are generally believed to be Master Kong's remarks, presenting the decrees and institutions of the ancient sage kings.

20.2 Zi-zhang asked Master Kong, saying: "What must we do to be able to engage in government?"

The Master said: "Uphold five virtues and eliminate four vices and you shall be able to engage in government."

Zi-zhang said: "What are the five virtues?"

The Master said: "The gentleman[1] is beneficent without being wasteful, capable of making the people toil without causing resentment, desirous without being greedy, self-possessed without being swaggering, and awesome without being fierce."

Zi-zhang said: "What do you mean by 'beneficent without being wasteful'?"

The Master said: "To profit the people where they can best be profited[2]—is it not 'beneficent without being wasteful'? To choose what they can do in making them toil[3]—who will then resent him? To desire humanity and attain humanity[4]—how can he be considered greedy? The gentleman dares slight neither the majority nor the minority, neither the small nor the great—is it not 'self-possessed without being swaggering'? The gentleman is correct in robe and hat, solemn in appearance and gaze, and looks so dignified that people gazing at him cannot help being awe-stricken—is it not 'awesome without being fierce'?"

Zi-zhang said: "What are the four vices?"

The Master said: "To kill without first instructing is called tyranny; to demand immediate completion without first giving warning is called impetuosity; to be slow in issuing orders but abrupt in setting time limits is called crookedness; in making indispensable payments to others, to be niggardly in the actual paying is called the way of a functionary."

1. Referring to a humane ruler or a humane minister of high rank.

2. To allow and help the people develop their economy by taking advantage of the natural resources in their respective living areas—for instance, to help those who live in mountains develop hunting and logging, those who live by seas, rivers, and lakes develop fishing and salt, and those who live on the central plains develop agriculture.

3. That is, to employ the peasants in such tasks as digging irrigation canals and ditches, earthworks, military training, etc. during winter time or other slack season in farming. Cf.1.5: "to employ the people at proper times."

4. That is, if he wishes to implement humane government and achieves it.

20.3 Master Kong said: "If one does not know the decree of Heaven, one has no way of becoming a gentleman;[1] if one does not know the rituals, one has no way of establishing oneself;[2] if one does not know speech, one has no way of knowing men."[3]

1. The decree of Heaven was generally believed by the ancients as well as by Master Kong to govern such matters as life and death, wealth and poverty, success and failure, and good fortune and adversity. (Cf., e.g., 6.10. 12.5, 14.36.) It is sometimes translated as "Fate."

2. Cf. 8.8, 16.13.

3. In listening to what a man says, one gets to know whether or not the speaker is a righteous man.

CHRONOLOGY OF CHINESE DYNASTIES

The Five Emperors (2550?–2140? B.C.E.)

Huang Di, or The Yellow Emperor
Zhuanxu
Di Ku, or Emperor Ku
Tang Yao
Yu Shun

Xia		2140?–1711? B.C.E.
Shang	(later changed to Yin)	1711?–1066? B.C.E.
Zhou	Western Zhou	1066?–771 B.C.E.
	Eastern Zhou	770–256 B.C.E.
	Spring and Autumn	722–481 B.C.E.
	Warring States	403–221 B.C.E.
Qin		221–206 B.C.E.
Han	Western Han	206 B.C.E.–25 A.D.
	Eastern Han	25–200
Three Kingdoms	Wei	220–265
	Shu Han	221–263
	Wu	222–280
Western Jin		265–317
Eastern Jin		317–420

Northern and Southern Dynasties	Southern Dynasties	Song	420–479
		Qi	479–502
		Liang	502–557
		Chen	557–589
	Northern Dynasties	Northern Wei	386–534
		Eastern Wei	534–550
		Northern Qi	550–577
		Western Wei	535–556
		Northern Zhou	557–581
Sui			581–618
Tang			618–907
Five Dynasties		Later Liang	907–923
		Later Tang	923–936
		Later Jin	936–947
		Later Han	947–950
		Later Zhou	951–960
Song		Northern Song	960–1127
		Southern Song	1127–1279
Liao			907–1125
Jin			1115–1234
Yuan			1206–1368
Ming			1368–1644
Qing			1616–1911

LIFE OF MASTER KONG

The only official biography of Master Kong is *Shi Ji, Kong Zi Shi Jia* (*Records of the Historiographer, The Hereditary House of Master Kong*) by the Han historiographer Si-ma Qian (145?–86 B.C.E.). It was long accepted as the standard work on the subject, but since the publication of *Zhu Si Kao Xin Lu* (*A study on the Authenticity of Confucian Literature*) by Cui Shu (1740–1816) in the Qing Dynasty, modern and contemporary scholars have become skeptical about its validity. For in *Shi Jia*, the historiographer has included a number of legends and myths of dubious sources in his writings. In the biography of Liu Bang, the founding father of the Han Dynasty, for example, he starts out by recounting the mythical tale that Liu Bang was born after his mother dreamt of meeting with a god and a dragon was seen hovering above her.[1]

Master Kong was regarded as a sage by many even when he was still alive, and legends were already circulating about his omniscience. During his lifetime none of the princes of the various states was particularly interested in his Way of humanity. After his death, however, he soon became a great favorite of the Han emperors, who, seeing the enormous advantage of his "loyalty to the sovereign" theory in strengthening their own imperial rule, officially conferred on him the title of "sage," and innumerable temples were dedicated to him all over the empire, thus making him a demigod. As a result, legends about him began to accumulate. By the time Si-ma Qian started to write the *Shi Jia*, there were quite a number of fantastic and legendary data he was obliged to take into account: that the Master's pate was concave in shape; that he was nine feet six inches tall; that on one occasion, he was able to identify a weird, sheep-like animal dug up from under a well as a dog; that on another, he was able to identify a huge section of a bone that filled a whole cart as part of the skeleton of Fang-feng Shi, one of the princes of states during the reign of the sage king Yu; that on a third, he was able to identify an arrow in a fallen falcon as belonging to the remote barbarian tribe Shu-shen to the northeast of

China proper; that on a fourth, he was able to identify as a kylin an outlandish animal captured on a wintry hunt; that he was promoted to the office of acting prime minister and that, on the seventh day of this promotion, he had the Lu minister Shao-zheng Mao executed; that on hearing in Chen that there had been a conflagration in Lu, he intuitively knew which ancestral temples of the ducal house had been burnt; and so on. However, that does not entitle us to discredit all the data presented in Si-ma Qian's work. For, in point of fact, the greater part of the events recorded in the *Shi Jia* are well documented in other historical and scholarly sources.

In my view, the sensible and scientific thing to do is to examine the data presented in the *Shi Jia* seriously, cast away those stories that are evidently legendary and unfounded, leave those that are questionable open, and preserve those that are substantially documented. Guided by this principle, I have reconstructed the brief life of Master Kong on the basis of those statements in the *Shi Jia* that are corroborated by one or more of these ancient texts:

1. *Zuo Zhuan, Gong-yang Zhuan*, and *Gu-liang Zhuan*, the three commentaries on the *Spring and Autumn Annals* (all in *Shi San Jing Zhu Shu*, or *Annotations and Interpretations on the Thirteen Classics*)
2. Chichung Huang, *The Analects of Confucius* (*Lun Yu*) (New York: Oxford University Press, 1997)
3. *D.C. Lau, Mencius* (London: Penguin Books, 1970)
4. *Han Fei Zi* (*Master Han Fei*), in *Bai Zi Quan Shu* (*Complete Works of a Hundred Masters*, Hangzhou: Zhejiang People's Press, 1985)
5. *Zhuang Zi* (*Master Zhuang*), in *Bai Zi Quan Shu*
6. *Kong Zi Jia Yu* (*Master Kong's Family Sayings*), in *Bai Zi Quan Shu*

Master Kong was born in Zou County, Chang-ping Prefecture, the State of Lu[2] in the twenty-first year of Duke Xiang's reign (552 B.C.E.)[3] toward the later part of the Zhou Dynasty, known as the Spring and Autumn period. His family was descended from the ducal house of the State of Song, which in turn was descended from the royal house of the Yin Dynasty.[4] Kong Fu-jia, his sixth-generation ancestor, who served as minister of military affairs to Duke Shang of Song, was assassinated along with the duke himself by Song's prime minister, Hua

Du, in a coup d'etat.⁵ To evade the persecution of the rival house of Hua, Fu-jia's son Mu Jin-fu⁶ moved the family from Song to the State of Lu, where they lived in obscurity for a number of generations until the Master's father, Shu-liang He, achieved some prominence, serving as magistrate of Zou County. While he was a minor officer in the battle against Bi-yang, Shu-liang distinguished himself by his remarkable physical strength and prowess.⁷ At around sixty years of age, he married a young girl named Yan Zheng-zai in disregard of the rituals.⁸ Zheng-zai gave birth to a son after the couple prayed at Mount Ni-qiu. Hence, the boy was bestowed the given name Qiu and the alias Zhong-ni.⁹

Shu-liang died soon after the boy was born, and the family was fast reduced to poverty. During his adolescence, Zhong-ni had to do various menial jobs to support his mother, who also died a little later. When he grew older, Zhong-ni held such insignificant positions as granary clerk and animal husbandry supervisor for the noble house of Ji-sun.¹⁰ At nineteen (534 B.C.E.), he married a daughter of the Jian-guan family in the State of Song, who bore him a son the following year and later a daughter, who married his disciple Gong-ye Chang.¹¹

Zhong-ni took to learning seriously at the age of fifteen (538 B.C.E.). Having no regular teachers, he learned from whoever possessed some knowledge of King Wen and King Wu's Way, that is, the rituals and music, two subjects of learning that played an important role in government during the Zhou Dynasty: He consulted the Viscount of Tan, prince of a vassal state of Lu who was on a state visit to Lu, on the practice of naming government offices after names of birds in Emperor Shao-hao's day;¹² Lao Dan, court librarian of the royal house of Zhou, on the rituals; and the Zhou minister Chang-hong on music. He learnt the musical composition *Succession* from the senior music master of Qi during his sojourn in that state and to play the zither from Music Master Xiang of Lu.

Master Kong must have distinguished himself as an authority on the rituals and statecraft early in his life, for at twenty-six (525 B.C.E.), he was already in a position to consult the visiting Viscount of Tan on the rituals; at twenty-nine (522 B.C.E.), he was so renowned that Duke Jing of Qi, a large state adjacent to Lu, and his prime minister Yan Ying, who were on a state visit to Lu, consulted him on the rituals and statecraft; at thirty-three (518 B.C.E.), the dying Meng Xi-zi, then head of the noble house of Meng-sun, urged his two sons, Meng Yi-zi and Nan-gong Jing-shu, to learn the rituals from him.[13] The Master himself also said: "I was established at thirty."[14]

We know very little about his life during the two decades that followed (523–503 B.C.E.), from when he was thirty to when he was fifty. What we do know is that he was well versed in the classics by thirty and had started a school, one of the very first private schools in Chinese history to accept the children of the poor and lowly[15] and that in 517 B.C.E., Duke Zhao of Lu, in an attempt to seize state power back from the three noble houses, attacked the dominant house of Ji-sun but was defeated by the allied forces of Ji-sun, Shu-sun, and Meng-sun and fled to Qi. Seeking refuge from the upheavals in Lu, Master Kong also escaped to Qi, where Duke Jing, although unable to employ him, often consulted him on the rituals and on statecraft. Subsequently, as his situation in Qi became more and more insecure, he was obliged to return to Lu. In 510 B.C.E., Duke Zhao died in the State of Jin and was succeeded by his younger brother, Duke Ding. In 505 B.C.E., Yang Huo, the rebellious house officer of Ji Huan-zi, who was then prime minister of Lu, took the latter into custody and began to control state affairs in Lu. Yang tried to persuade Master Kong to take office, but the Master devoted himself to teaching school and editing the classics instead.[16] His school flourished, and students were coming in large numbers, many from distant foreign states. In 502 B.C.E., Yang Huo rebelled openly, was defeated, and fled, first to Qi, and later to Jin, where he settled down.[17]

In the ninth year of Duke Ding's reign (501 B.C.E.), when the Master was fifty, the duke appointed him magistrate of Zhong-du.[18] Thereafter, accompanied by his disciple Nan-gong Jing-shu, the Master went to visit the royal court of Zhou, where he consulted Lao Zi on the rituals and Chang Hong on music.[19] The next year (500 B.C.E.), he was promoted first to the position of deputy minister of public works and then to the post of minister of justice[20] in recognition of his accomplishments in Zhong-du. Later that year, Qi and Lu convened at Jia-gu a meeting to promote peace and friendship at which Master Kong served as master of ceremonies. During the meeting, the authorities of Qi made an attempt to abduct Duke Ding by force but were defeated and renounced by Master Kong in accordance with the rituals. Duke Jing of Qi then offered his apologies and returned to Lu the land of Yun and Huan as well as that lying north of Mount Tortoise, which Qi had annexed from Lu in times past.[21]

In the twelfth year of Duke Ding's reign (498 B.C.E.), Master Kong, in an attempt to weaken the three noble houses that controlled state power and to strengthen the power of the ducal house of Lu, proposed to the duke that the extra-long city walls of the three noble lords' fiefs be demolished. With the duke's approval, the Master gave orders to his disciple Zi-lu, then chief house officer to Ji Huan-zi, to put the decree into execution. The demolition of the city walls of Shu-sun's fief Hou and Ji-sun's fief Bi went smoothly enough, but when it came to Meng-sun's fief Cheng, Meng Yi-zi declined to comply, and a battle ensued. The duke's army besieged Cheng but was unable to capture it. Thus the whole strategy was foiled.[22]

With Master Kong's participation in government, Lu became remarkably well ruled. This constituted a potential menace and a cause for concern to the authorities of its neighboring state Qi. On the proposition of his minister Li Chu, Duke Jing of Qi presented to Duke Ding of Lu a troupe of singing girls and thirty teams of colorfully draped horses. His intention was, of course, to corrupt the court of Lu and to defeat the Master's efforts to revitalize its government. The duke and Ji Huan-zi accepted the gifts readily and indulged themselves in the beautiful girls, as well as in their singing. For many days thereafter, court meetings were suspended. A little later, a state sacrifice to Heaven was observed in the suburbs of Qu-fu, capital of Lu, and the sacrificial meat was not distributed to the participating ministers as prescribed by the rituals. At that point, the Master left office and departed from Lu in the thirteenth year of Duke Ding's reign (497 B.C.E.).[23]

Thus began fourteen years of fruitless and adventurous travels for the Master and his retinue, a group of his disciples, as they searched for a wise prince who would employ him and allow him to implement the sage kings' Way of government. During those fourteen years, the Master had audiences with the princes of various states, but none showed any genuine interest in his political theory or gave him any office of substantial power to implement it.

The first state the Master and his retinue visited was Wei, whose reigning prince, Duke Ling, was a generous host to his distinguished guest. But military force and women being the duke's dominating passions, he was not at all interested in the Master's theory of humane government. As Master Kong had befriended such worthy men as Qu Bo-yu among its ministers, however, and as a number of his disciples had taken office in its court, he more or less made Wei his base, a place he returned to repeatedly when his search elsewhere was unsuccessful. When Duke Ling died, his grandson, Duke Chu, succeeded to the throne because his son, Crown Prince Kuai-kui, was in exile. As many of the Master's disciples were serving in his court, the young duke once contemplated employing the Master as his aide. But again, this did not transpire.[24]

The next state the Master's party visited was Chen. On the way there, they were besieged by the natives of Kuang[25] due to Master Kong's resemblance to Yang Huo, who had brutalized the people of Kuang in times past. When the Master and his followers finally managed to arrive in Chen, Duke Min of Chen granted the Master a nominal position. The Master and his followers had been in Chen for three years or so when Wu invaded Chen, and they were obliged to leave Chen for Cai. During their journey, they ran out of food for seven days, and the Masters' faithful disciples Zi-lu and Zi-gong almost lost their faith in the Master's cause.[26]

When the Master and his disciples were in great adversity between Chen and Cai, King Zhao of Chu, who earnestly wished to engage the Master, dispatched an army to escort him and his party to Chu. The king wanted to grant him a fief and a position in his court, but it did not happen due to the intervention of Zi-xi, Chu's prime minister. During his stay in Chu, the Master met with Duke of She, a worthy minister of that state, who consulted him on statecraft and on the rituals.[27]

The party then departed for the State of Song. One day during their sojourn there, the Master and his disciples were practicing the rituals under a big tree. Huan Tui, Song's minister of military affairs, who was intent upon killing the Master, had the tree uprooted. Eventually, the Master managed to flee Song in disguise.[28]

In the autumn of 492 B.C.E., Ji Huan-zi, very sick, urged his heir, Kang-zi, to summon Master Kong back to Lu when Kang-zi succeeded him as prime minister. However, Kang-zi recalled the Master's disciple Ran Qiu, instead. The Master, now around sixty, missed his homeland very much.

In 484 B.C.E., his disciple Ran Qiu led an army in behalf of Ji Kang-zi and defeated the invading forces of Qi.[29] At Ran Qiu's recommendation and Ji Kang-zi's request, Master Kong finally returned to Lu in the eleventh year of Duke Ai's reign (484 B.C.E.), when the

Master was sixty-seven. After his return to Lu, Duke Ai and Ji Kang-zi frequently consulted him on state affairs; yet they had no intention of employing him, nor was he anxious to take office now, prefering to spend the remaining years of his life arranging, editing, commenting on, and transmitting the classics.

In the fourteenth year of Duke Ai's reign (481 B.C.E.), Chen Heng, a minister of Qi, assassinated his sovereign lord, Duke Jian. The Master reported the incident to the duke and the three lords, requesting that a punitive expedition be sent against the culprit. But his proposal was not approved.

During the last years of his life, the Master was a solitary and heartbroken old man. Those who were dear to him departed from the world one after another. His wife died in 485 B.C.E., one year before his return to Lu; his only son, Li, died in 482 B.C.E., two years after his return; the following year (481 B.C.E.) saw the untimely death of his favorite disciple, Yan Hui; the year after that (480 B.C.E.), his most faithful disciple, Zi-lu, was killed in the civil strife in Wei. Desolate and weighed down by grief, Master Kong himself died in the sixteenth year of Duke Ai's reign (479 B.C.E.), at the age of seventy-two. He was buried by River Si, north of Qu-fu. Greatly saddened by the Master's death, the disciples observed "heart mourning"[30] for three years, at the end of which they parted in grief. Zi-gong alone remained and mourned three more years for his master in a shed built at the Master's grave for that purpose.

Master Kong begot Li, alias Bo-yu; Li begot Ji, alias Zi-si. . . . Beginning with the Master, the house of the Kongs has seen seventy-seven generations up to the present day.[31]

NOTES

1. See *Shi Ji, Gao Zu Ben Ji (Records of the Historiographer, The Founding Father's Annals)*, vol. VIII, p. 341.

2. The State of Lu was situated in the southwestern part of the present Shandong Province, with Qu-fu (where the present-day Qu-fu is) as its capital; both the prefecture and the county were southeast of Qu-fu.

3. *Gong-yang Zhuan* and *Gu-liang Zhuan* both place the Master's birth in the twenty-first year of Duke Xiang's reign, 552 B.C.E. (see *Shi San Jing Zhu Shu*, pp. 2309 and 2430, respectively), whereas *Kong Zi Shi Jia* has it in the twenty-second year of Duke Xiang's reign (551 B.C.E.)

4. Master Kong was descended from the Viscount of Wei, founding father of the State of Song, who was half brother to King Zhou, the last emperor of the Yin Dynasty—see "Family Tree of the Kongs" and *Lun Yu*, 18.1, note 1; also see *Zuo Zhuan, Duke Zhao*, 7th year (see *Shi San Jing Zhu Shu*, p. 2051) and *Kong Zi Jia Yu*, ch. 42, p. 1 (*Bai Zi Quan Shu*, Tome I).

5. See *Zuo Zhuan, Gong-yang Zhuan*, and *Gu-liang Zhuan* (*Shi San Jing Zhu Shu*, pp. 1740, 2213, and 2372, respectively). See also *Zuo Zhuan*, Duke Zhao, 7th year (*Shi San Jing Zhu Shu*, p. 2051).

6. Some scholars believe it was Fang-shu, Fu-jia's great grandson, who fled to Lu.

7. See *Zuo Zhuan*, Duke Xiang, 10th year (*Shi San Jing Zhu Shu*, p. 1946). Bi-yang was a small state of the Spring and Autumn period, south of the present-day Zao-zhuang, Shandong Province. The battle against Bi-yang was fought between the allied forces of various states and the State of Bi-yang, which was eventually defeated and exterminated by its enemies. During the siege of Bi-yang, the gate of the city suddenly opened. After many soldiers of the allied forces charged into the city, the portcullis was abruptly lowered. By sheer physical strength and prowess, Shu-liang, a minor officer of the Lu army, lifted and held the portcullis with his bare hands so that the trapped men were able to make their escape.

Note that Shu-liang was Master Kong's father's alias and He, his given name. In ancient times, a man was often referred to by a name that was the combination of his alias and his given name without including the family name.

8. Si-ma Qian used the phrase *ye he* to describe Shu-liang's relation with Zheng-zai. The reading of *ye he* has been controversial for centuries. Ancient scholars read it as "married in violation of the rituals" because Shu-liang was past sixty, whereas Zheng-zai was not yet twenty; contemporary scholars, how-ever, read it as "had an illicit relation"; in other words, according to this reading, Master Kong was the natural son of his parents. The ancient con-notation of the character *ye* is "simple, uncultured, or not knowing the rituals," which can still be found in the classical lexicon. *Sea of Words (Ci Hai)*; Actually, the classical lexicon *Sources of Words (Ci Yuan)* literally defines the phrase "ye he" as "to marry (or a marriage) in disregard of the rituals." In all the three instances where *ye* occurs in *Lun Yu*, the idea "not knowing the rituals" is implied. (See *Lun Yu*, 6.18, 11.1, 13.3.)

9. It is self-evident that his name, Qiu, and his alias, Zhong-ni ("Zhong" implies second son) are closely related to the name of Mount Ni-qiu, which is southeast of the present-day Qu-fu, then capital of Lu.

10. The most powerful of the three noble houses that were in control of state power in Lu.

11. See *Lun Yu*, 5.1.

12. See *Zuo Zhuan, Duke Zhao*, 17th year (525 B.C.E.) (see *Shi San Jing Zhu Shu*, pp. 2082–2084).

13. See *Zuo Zhuan, Duke Zhao*, 7th year (see *Shi San Jing Zhu Shu*, p. 2051).

14. See *Lun Yu*, 2.4. Note that "to be established" here means "to be well cultivated in the rituals," or "to stand firmly on the rituals."

15. See *Lun Yu* 6.11, 7.7, 9.27, 15.39, etc. Such disciples as Yan Hui, Zi-lu, Zhong-gong, Yuan Xian, and Zeng Shen all came from poor and lowly families.

16. See *Lun Yu*, 17.1.

17. See *Zuo Zhuan, Duke Ding*, 9th year (*Shi San Jing Zhu Shu*, p. 2144).

18. County of Lu, west of the present-day Wen-shang, Shandong Province. See *Kong Zi Jia Yu*, ch. 1, p. 1 (*Bai Zi Quan Shu*, Tome I).

19. See *Zhuang Zi*, ch. 14, pp. 11–12 (*Bai Zi Quan Shu*, Tome VIII), and *Kong Zi Jia Yu*, ch. 11, p. 1 (*Bai Zi Quan Shu*, Tome I). The date of the trip to the royal court of Zhou is unascertainable.

20. That Master Kong served as minister of justice in Lu is recorded in *Zuo Zhuan, Duke Ding*, 1st year (*Shi San Jing Zhu Shu*, p. 2132) and in *Mencius*, VI.B.6. (D.C. Lau translated *Si Kou* as police commissioner.) *Kong Zi Jia Yu* mentions it numerous times. In several chapters of *Lun Yu*, Master Kong himself said he had once followed in the wake of the ministers, an humble way of saying that he once served as a minister in Lu.

21. The incident at Jia-gu is recorded in all three commentaries in *The Spring and Autumn Annals* (see *Shi San Jing Zhu Shu*, pp. 2147–2148, 2341, and 2445, respectively).

Jia-gu—a county of Qi, east of the present-day Lai-wu, Shandong Province

Yun—a county of Lu, east of the present-day Yun City, Shandong Province

Huan—a county of Lu, south of the present-day Fei City, Shandong Province

Mount Tortoise—northeast of the present-day Si-shui, Shandong Province

22. See *Zuo Zhuan, Gong-yang Zhuan*, and *Gu-liang Zhuan*, Duke Ding, 12th year (*Shi San Jing Zhu Shu*, pp. 2149, 2342, 2445–2446, respectively).

23. See *Lun Yu*, 18.4; *Mencius*, VI.B.6; *Kong Zi Jia Yu*, ch. 19, p. 3 (*Bai Zi Quan Shu*, Tome I), and *Han Fei Zi*, ch. 31, p. 5 (*Bai Zi Quan Shu*, Tome III).

24. The chapters in *Lun Yu* that record Master Kong's visits to Wei include 3.13, 6.28, 7.15, 9.5, 9.18, 13.3, 13.9, 15.1, 15.7.

25. See *Lun Yu*, 9.5, and *Kong Zi Jia Yu*, ch. 22, p. 6 (*Bai Zi Quan Shu*, Tome I). Kuang was a county of Wei, southwest of what is now Chang-yuan, Henan Province. There is still a Kuang City some five miles southwest of Chang-yuan, which might have been the place where Master Kong was besieged.

26. See *Lun Yu*, 15.2; *Kong Zi Jia Yu*, chs. 20, 22, pp. 3 & 5 (*Bai Zi Quan Shu*, Tome I).

27. See *Lun Yu*, 13.16, 13.18.

28. See *Lun Yu*, 7.22; *Mencius*, V.A.8.

Li Ji, Tan Gong carries the following story: When Master Kong lived in Song, Huan Tui, Song's minister of military affairs, was having a stone outer coffin made for himself. It was not finished after three whole years. The Master said: "How prodigal that man is! It would be better for a man to rot faster after death" (see *Shi San Jing Zhu Shu*, p. 1290). That might have been the cause of Huan's desire to kill the Master.

29. See *Zuo Zhuan, Duke Ai*, 11th year (see *Shi San Jing Zhu Shu*, p. 2166), and *Kong Zi Jia Yu*, ch. 38, p. 1 (*Bai Zi Quan Shu*, Tome I).

30. According to *Li Ji* (*Records of the Rituals*), when one's teacher dies, one should mourn him for three years with the same genuine grief as that with which one mourns one's father, only without the mourning apparel. This is called "heart mourning" (see *Shi San Jing Zhu Shu*, p. 1274).

31. Master Kong's seventy-seventh-generation descendant is Kong De-cheng, ex-minister of examination in Taiwan.

MASTER KONG'S MAJOR DISCIPLES

This collection of biographies, based on *Shi Ji, Zhong-ni Di Zi Lie Zhuan* (*Records of the Historiographer, Biographies of Zhong-ni's Disciples*) in collation with *Kong Zi Shi Jia, Kong Zi Jia Yu,* and *Lun Yu,* includes only those disciples who appear in *Lun Yu.*

Lun Yu, 11.3 says: "Moral conduct: Yan Yuan, Min Zi-qian, Ran Bo-niu, and Zhong-gong; speech: Zai Wo and Zi-gong; state affairs: Ran You and Ji-lu; literature: Zi-you and Zi-xia." This is a list of the disciples who excelled in the four branches of learning at the Master's school. It is the order followed by Si-ma Qian in compiling his *Zhong-ni Di Zi Lie Zhuan* (at least in the case of the leading ten); so is it the order followed here.

---

1. **Yan Hui** (521?–481 B.C.E.), alias Zi-yuan, also known as Yan Yuan, one of the Master's most prominent disciples in the early part of his teaching career,[1] also one of those who followed him in his travels abroad; son of Yan Lu, who was one of the earliest disciples at the Master's school; native of Lu. Humane by nature and well accomplished both in virtue and the classics, he delighted in pursuing the Way even when in dire straits. The top disciple among those who excelled in moral conduct at the Master's school, he was the only one commended by the Master as a humane man and considered fit to succeed him in transmitting and implementing the Way of humanity. His hair went white when he was twenty-nine, and he died at the young age of thirty-one. The Master lamented him grievously.

2. **Min Sun** (536 B.C.E.–?), alias Zi-qian, one of the Master's prominent disciples in the early part of his teaching career and the second best among those who excelled in moral conduct at his school; native of Lu. He was well known for keeping his family in harmony and commended highly by the Master for his filial piety and for declining to take office in the noble house of Ji-sun, who was a usurper of state power.[2]

3. **Ran Geng** (544 B.C.E.–?), alias Bo-niu, one of the Master's prominent disciples in the early part of his teaching career; the third best

in the category of disciples who excelled in moral conduct; native of Lu. When the Master was serving as minister of justice in Lu, Bo-niu was appointed magistrate of Zhong-du. Subsequently he contracted a foul disease and died young. The master felt great pain at losing him.

4. **Ran Yong** (522 B.C.E.–?), alias Zhong-gong, one of the Master's prominent disciples in the early part of his teaching career; native of Lu. Born of an unworthy father, he excelled in moral conduct, for which Master Kong thought highly of him, considering him fit to rule a state as a prince. After finishing school, he once served as chief officer in the noble house of Ji-sun.

5. **Zai Yu**, alias Zi-wo, generally known as Zai Wo, dates unknown, one of the Master's major disciples in the early part of his teaching career and the foremost among the disciples who excelled in speech; native of Lu. He was severely criticized by the Master for proposing to reduce the three-year mourning term for one's parents to one year and for sleeping during the day. He first served as minister of Lin-zi[3] in the State of Qi, but was eventually killed and the three clans[4] closest to him exterminated on account of his involvement in Chen Heng's rebellion.[5]

6. **Duan-mu Ci** (520 B.C.E.–?), alias Zi-gong, one of the Master's most prominent and faithful disciples in the early part of his teaching career, also one of those who followed him in his travels abroad; native of the State of Wei. The second best among those who excelled in speech at the Master's school, he later became a renowned diplomat. Often representing Lu as an envoy to foreign lands, sometimes he was able to change the political situation in the entire empire. He later served as prime minister to Lu and then to Wei. Being also conversant with trade, he eventually became very wealthy. When Master Kong died, he mourned him for six years in a hut built at the Master's grave. He was a staunch defender of his master when others maligned him. He himself died in the State of Qi.

7. **Ran Qiu** (522 B.C.E.–?), alias Zi-you, generally known as Ran You, one of the Master's prominent disciples in the early part of his teaching career, also one of those who followed him in his travels abroad; native of Lu. Talented and versatile, he was foremost among the disciples who excelled in statecraft at the Master's school. He once served as chief house officer in the noble house of Ji-sun, but was criticized severely by the Master for amassing wealth for his lord and for his inability to prevent Ji Kang-zi from attacking Lu's vassal state,

Zhuan-yu. In 484 B.C.E., he was made commander of a resistance army and defeated the invading forces of Qi. It was on his recommendation that Ji Kang-zi finally invited Master Kong to return to his native land after fourteen years of travels abroad.

8. Zhong lou (542–480 B.C.E.), alias Zi-lu and Ji-lu, one of the Master's earliest, closest, most faithful, and most prominent disciples, also one of those who followed him in his travels abroad; native of Lu's Bian County. He was the second best disciple among those who excelled in statecraft. Noted for his courage and his sense of justice, he was true to his word and eager to practice what he had learned. Versed in government, he served first as house officer in the noble house of Ji-sun and later as magistrate of the Wei minister Kong Kui's fief. He was eventually killed in the internal strife in that state.

9. Yan Yan (506 B.C.E.–?), alias Zi-you, also known as Yan You, one of the Master's prominent disciples in the later part of his teaching career[6] and the best of those who excelled in the classics; native of the State of Wu. *Lun Yu* contains four Chapters of his sayings. After graduating from Master Kong's school, he served as magistrate of Wu City, where he endeavored to govern by the rituals and music. He later started a school of his own to transmit Master Kong's teachings.

10. Bu Shang (507 B.C.E.–?), alias Zi-xia, one of the Master's prominent disciples in the later part of his teaching career; native of Wei. *Lun Yu* contains thirteen chapters of his sayings. He was versed in the classics, especially in *The Book of Poetry*. After finishing school, he served as magistrate of Ju-fu County[7] in Lu. When the Master died, he went to teach school at West River,[8] where he once served as court tutor to the studious Marquis Wen of Wei (r. 445–396 B.C.E.).[9] He became one of the major transmitters of the Ru School, transmitting *The Book of Poetry*, *The Book of Changes*, *The Spring and Autumn Annals*, and *The Book of Rituals*. Later in his life, when his son died, he grieved so inconsolably that he lost his eyesight.

11. Zhuan-sun Shi (503 B.C.E.–?), alias Zi-zhang, one of the Master's prominent disciples in the early part of his teaching career; also one of those who followed him in his travels abroad; native of Chen. *Lun Yu* contains three chapters of his sayings. He was versed in practicing the rituals, especially in appearance and deportment, but fell short in the pursuit of humanity. Later, he started a school of his own, and, on the basis of his teachings, his followers formed a branch of the Ru School known as "Zi-zhang's Sect of the Ru School."[10]

12. **Zeng Shen** (505–435 B.C.E.), alias Zi-yu, one of the most prominent disciples in the later part of the Master's teaching career; consistently referred to as Master Zeng in *Lun Yu*, which contains twelve and a half chapters of his sayings; native of South Wu City[11] in Lu; son of Zeng Dian, who was one of the Master's earliest disciples. Noted for his filial piety, the authorship of such works of the Ru School as *Master Zeng*, *The Book of Filial Piety*, and *Great Learning* were attributed to him. He later started a school of his own and became the first of a direct line of orthodox transmitters in the tradition of the Ru School, passing on the Master's Way to Zi-si, Master Kong's grandson, who, in turn, passed it on to Meng Ke (Mencius).

13. **Dan-tai Mie-ming** (512 B.C.E.–?), alias Zi-yu, one of the Master's major disciples in the later part of his teaching career; native of Wu City in Lu. He was very ugly in appearance, and the Master considered him deficient in natural endowments. Having graduated from the Master's school, he applied himself to moral self-cultivation and proved to be an upright and reliable person. Subsequently, he traveled to the Yangtze River region where he started a school of his own, and had a following of 300 students. Eventually, he became one of the major transmitters of the Ru School, and made quite a name for himself among the princes of the various states. Upon hearing this, Master Kong said regretfully: "I used to judge a person by his speech and erred in Zai Yu; I used to judge a person by his appearance and erred in Zi-yu."[12]

14. **Fu Bu-qi** (521 B.C.E.–?), alias Zi-jian, one of the Master's major disciples in the early part of his teaching career; native of Lu. When he served as magistrate of Shan-fu County[13] in Lu, the county was well ruled while he played the zither. The Master commended him, saying that his capacity was fit to serve as a king's, or an overlord's aide.

15. **Yuan Xian** (515 B.C.E.–?), alias Zi-si, also known as Yuan Si, one of the Master's major disciples in the early part of his teaching career; native of Lu. When Master Kong was minister of justice, Xian served as his chief house officer. After the Master's death, Xian retired to the State of Wei, where he lived in seclusion. He was one of those disciples who delighted in pursuing the Way and in preserving his integrity even in poverty.

16. **Gong-ye Chang**, alias Zi-chang, dates unknown, one of the Master's major disciples in the early period of his teaching career; native

of Qi. Although he was once imprisoned, the Master had faith in his integrity and married his daughter to him.

17. **Meng Yi-zi**, originally named Zhong-sun He-ji, dates unknown eldest son of Meng Xi-zi and elder brother of Nan-gong Kuo, head of the noble house of Meng-sun after his father's death; native of Lu. His name is not included in *Shi Ji Kong Zi Jia Yu*, but *Zuo Zhuan, Duke Zhao*, 7th year, clearly says: "Therefore, Meng Yi-zi and Nan-gong Jing-shu served Master Kong as their teacher" (see *Shi San Jing Zhu Shu*, p. 2051). He was a treacherous student, for it was he who defeated the Master's plan to demolish the extra-long city walls of the three noble houses fiefs by refusing to comply and fighting against Duke Ding's besieging army. (See the section on life of Master Kong, p. 195.)

18. **Nan-gong Kuo**, alias Zi-rong, generally known as Nan Rong, also known as Nan-gong Tao and Nan-gong Jing-shu, younger son of Meng Xi-zi, and younger brother of Meng Yi-zi; original name was Zhong-sun Yue; dates unknown; one of the Master's major disciples in the early part of his teaching career; native of Lu. His father admired Master Kong's accomplishments in the rituals and urged his two sons to serve him as their teacher, which they did after their father's death. Commending Nan-gong Kuo as a gentleman who upheld virtue, the Master gave his elder brother's daughter to him in marriage. It was on his recommendation and in his company that the Master paid the visit to the royal court of the Zhou Dynasty to broaden his knowledge of the rituals and music.

19. **Zeng Dian** (546 B.C.E.–?), alias Zi-xi, also known as Zeng Xi, father to Zeng Shen, one of the Master's earliest disciples; five years younger than the Master, native of South Wu City in Lu. The Master commended him highly for aspiring to further cultivate himself in the rituals and music during the chaotic period in which he lived.

20. **Yan Wu-you** (545 B.C.E.–?), alias Ji-lu, or Lu, also known as Yan Lu; father to Yan Hui, six years younger than the Master, one of the earliest disciples at the Master's school; native of Lu.

21. **Gao Cai** (521 B.C.E.–?), alias Zi-gao, one of the Master's major disciples in the early part of his teaching; member of a branch of the noble house of Gao; career; native of Qi less than six feet tall, very ugly, and considered dull-witted by the Master. But actually, he was very resourceful. He first served in Lu as magistrate of Wu City and

later served in the court of Wei together with Zi-lu. In a coup d'etat there, Zi-gao managed to flee Wei in safety, but Zi-lu was killed in the civil strife.

22. Qi-diao Kai (540 B.C.E.–?), alias Zi-kai and Zi-rao, eleven years younger than the Master, one of the Master's major disciples in the early part of his teaching career; native of Cai. He learned *The Book of History* from the Master and was reluctant to take office before he was confident of his own cultivation, which pleased the Master very much.

23. Gong-bo Liao, alias Zi-zhou, native of Lu. *Lun Yu* records him as having informed against Zi-lu to Ji-sun. Not much is known about him.

24. Si-ma Geng, alias Zi-niu, generally known as Si-ma Niu, dates unknown, one of the Master's major disciples in the later part of his teaching career; younger brother of Huan Tui, Song's minister of military affairs; native of Song. Niu was constantly fearful and anxious because Huan Tui was planning to stage a revolt in Song. Niu was restless and talkative.

25. Fan Xu (515 B.C.E.–?), alias Zi-chi, generally known as Fan Chi, thirty-six years younger than the Master, one of the Master's major disciples in the early part of his teaching career; native of Qi. He once served as house officer in the noble house of Ji-sun. During the battle of Qing, he rendered meritorious services in helping his schoolmate/commander Ran You to rout the army of Qi.

26. You Ruo (508 B.C.E.–?), alias Zi-you, often respectfully referred to as Master You in *Lun Yu*, which carries four chapters of his sayings, forty-three years younger than the Master, one of the Master's prominent disciples in the later part of his teaching career; native of Lu. He was endowed with a remarkably good memory and loved antiquity. After the Master's death, the disciples missed him terribly. As You Ruo bore some resemblance to the Master in appearance, they set him up as their master and served him with the same respect they had shown Master Kong. As Zeng Shen opposed the idea, however, they finally gave up the practice.

27. Gong-xi Chi (509 B.C.E.–?), alias Zi-hua, generally known as Gong-xi Hua, forty-two years younger than the Master, one of the Master's major disciples in the later part of his teaching career; native of Lu. Versed in diplomacy, he often served Lu as envoy to other states.

28. Wu-ma Shi (521 B.C.E.–?), alias Zi-qi, generally known as Wu-ma Qi, thirty years younger than the Master, one of the Master's major disciples in the early part of his teaching career; native of Chen. Once he also served as magistrate of Shanfu County. He went out with the stars, came home with the stars and the county became well ruled.

29. Chen Kang (511 B.C.E.–?), alias Zi-qin, forty years younger than the Master, one of the Master's major disciples in the early part of his teaching career; native of Chen. He seemed quite blind to the magnitude of his master's learning.

30. Lin Fang, one of the Master's major disciples in the early part of his teaching career; little is known about him.

31. Qin Lao, alias Zi-kai and Zi-zhang, also known as Qin Zhang, dates unknown, one of the Master's major disciples in the early part of his teaching career; native of Wei.

32. Shen Cheng, alias Zhou, or Zi-zhou, dates unknown; native of Lu. Master Kong criticized him as being lustful.

33. Zi-fu He, alias Jing-bo; one of the Master's disciples in the early part of his teaching career; native of Lu. Not much is known about him.

34. Ru Bei, native of Lu. He was sent by Duke Ai to learn the mourning rituals of the *shi* from the Master.[14]

35. Kong Li (532–483 B.C.E.), alias Bo-yu, Master Kong's son, one of his major disciples in the early part of his teaching career;[15] native of Lu. When he was born, Duke Zhao of Lu presented the Master with a gift of carp. Feeling honored by the sovereign's favor, he gave his son the name Li (carp) and the alias Bo-yu (eldest + fish). He appears in two chapters of *Lun Yu* (Chs. 11.8 & 16.13) and died three years earlier than his father.

NOTES

1. Roughly from 522 B.C.E. to 497 B.C.E. (when the Master was 30 to 55), before he started his travels abroad.

2. See *Lun Yu*, 11.5, note 1, and 6.9.

3. Then capital of Qi. The city is still called Lin-zi today.

4. That is, one's father's clan, mother's clan, and wife's clan.

5. Also known as Chen Cheng-zi and Tian Chang. The rebellion cited here refers to Chen Heng's assassination of Duke Jian of Qi in *Lun Yu*, 14.21.

6. Roughly, from the year of the Master's return to Lu (484 B.C.E.) to the year of his death (479 B.C.E.).

7. A county of Lu, what is now Ju County, Shandong Province.

8. What is now An-yang, Henan Province, then a county of the State of Wei (in the present-day Shanxi Province, to be distinguished from the Wei in the present-day Henan Province), so-called because it was located to the west of the Yellow River.

9. Founder of the State of Wei (in Shanxi), named Wei Si. By employing capable ministers, promoting agriculture and warfare, encouraging learning, and implementing reforms, he was able to make Wei a culturally flourishing and powerful state of his day.

10. *Han Fei Zi, Xian Xue* (*Master Han Fei*, ch, 50: *Distinguished Schools*), p. 4: "After Master Kong's death, the Ru School comprised Zi-zhang's Sect, Zi-si's [the Master's grandson] Sect, Yan Shi's [Yan Hui] Sect, Meng Shi's [Meng Ke, or Mencius] Sect, Qi-diao Shi's [the Master's disciple Qi-diao Kai] Sect, Zhong-liang Shi's [the Master's disciple Gong-liang Ru?] Sect, Sun Shi's [the Master's disciple Gong-sun Long?] Sect, and Yue-Zheng Shi's [Zeng Shen's student Yue-zheng Zi-chun] Sect" (*Bai Zi Quan Shu*, Tome III).

11. County of Lu; in what is now Bi County, Shandong Province.

12. The Master considered Zai Wo (Yu) a well-cultivated disciple, judging by his speech, but the latter became a rebel who implicated the lives of the three clans that were closest to him; he considered Dan-tai Mie-ming untalented, judging by his ugliness, but he turned out to be an upright gentleman. Hence the Master's self-criticism.

13. South of the present-day Shan County, Shandong Province.

14. *Li Ji, Za Ji* (*Records of the Rituals, Records of Miscellaneous Matters*) says: "On Xu You's death, Duke Ai sent Ru Bei to Master Kong to learn the mourning rituals. *The Rituals Governing the Mourning of Shi* was thus rewritten" (see *Shi San Jing Zhu Shu*, p. 1567).

15. *Shi Ji, Zhong-ni Di Zi Lie Zhuan*, and *Kong Zi Jia Yu* do not include the Master's own son, Bo-yu, as one of his disciples. But judging from *Lun Yu*, 16.13, he apparently was one of them.

INDEX